RAY ALLAN
HENRY COMPTON SCHOOL, FULHAM, LONDON

MARTIN WILLIAMS
GEORGE MITCHELL SCHOOL, LEYTON, LONDON

OXFORD

OXFORD
UNIVERSITY PRESS

Great Clarendon Street, Oxford OX2 6DP

Oxford University Press is a department of the University of Oxford.
It furthers the University's objective of excellence in research, scholarship, and
education by publishing worldwide in

Oxford   New York

Auckland   Cape Town   Dar es Salaam   Hong Kong   Karachi
Kuala Lumpur   Madrid   Melbourne   Mexico City   Nairobi
New Delhi   Shanghai   Taipei   Toronto

With offices in

Argentina   Austria   Brazil   Chile   Czech Republic   France   Greece
Guatemala   Hungary   Italy   Japan   Poland   Portugal   Singapore
South Korea   Switzerland   Thailand   Turkey   Ukraine   Vietnam

Oxford is a registered trade mark of Oxford University Press
in the UK and in certain other countries

Oxford is a registered trade mark of Oxford University Press
in the UK and in certain other countries

First published 2001

10   9   8

British Library Cataloguing in Publication Data

Data available

ISBN-13: 978 0 19 914775 5

ISBN-10: 0-19-914775-2

Typeset by TechSet Ltd. Gateshead, Tyne and Wear.
Printed in Hong Kong

ABOUT THIS BOOK

Mathswise Book 2 is the second in a series of three books spanning levels 1 – 4 of the National Curriculum in England and Wales. It is aimed at students in year 8.

It has been written to give you plenty of practice at the basic concepts in mathematics so you can build up confidence and achieve your best level in the Key Stage 3 tests at the end of year 9.

The authors have many years teaching experience at this level and all the activities and exercises in this book are built on their considerable knowledge of what students in year 8 are able to understand.

Each unit in the book starts with the **learning outcomes** of the unit so that you can see what you are expected to learn.

There is a box highlighting key mathematical words

Examples are often given to show you how to approach questions. They are in blue shaded boxes, for example:

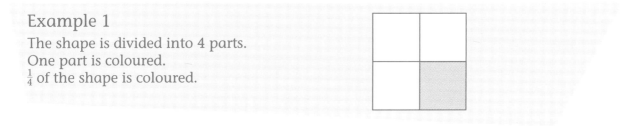

Example 1
The shape is divided into 4 parts.
One part is coloured.
$\frac{1}{4}$ of the shape is coloured.

This icon highlights Numeracy focus pages. These pages encourage numeracy practice in other contexts.

There are regular **revision exercises** throughout the book. Make sure you can do the revision questions before you move on to the next unit.

At the end of the book there is a section called **Street Maths**. This section allows you to practise all the skills you have learnt in the book. This means you can be sure you understand the concepts before moving on to the next book in the series.

The **answers** to the exercises in the book are available in a separate book from the publishers. See the back cover for details.

Contents

1 FRACTIONS

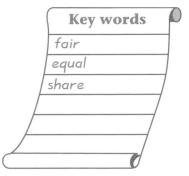

Key words
fair
equal
share

This unit will help you to:
→ **identify unit and non-unit fractions**
→ **find $\frac{1}{2}$s, $\frac{1}{3}$s, $\frac{1}{4}$s, $\frac{1}{5}$s**
→ **identify identical fractions.**

FAIR SHARES

Steve and Roger are sharing a cake.
Steve cuts it into two pieces.
But, as you can see the pieces are
not equal. . . . So:

Exercise 1

1. A cake has been shared three ways. Which drawing shows fair shares?

a  **b**  **c**

2. A block of ice cream is shared two ways. Which drawing shows fair shares?

a  **b**  **c**

3. A cake has been shared four ways. Which drawing shows fair shares?

a  **b**  **c**

4. A block of fudge is shared six ways. Which drawing shows fair shares?

a 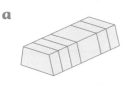 **b**  **c**

SHARING

When 4 friends share a cake, each person will get $\frac{1}{4}$ of the cake.

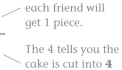

The 1 tells you each friend will get 1 piece.

The 4 tells you the cake is cut into **4 equal parts**.

$\frac{1}{4}$ $\frac{1}{4}$ $\frac{1}{4}$ $\frac{1}{4}$

Exercise 2

By looking at the cake, or the number of friends in each drawing below, say what fraction of the cake each person will get.

1.

2.

3.

4.

5.

6.

7.

8.

NAMES OF FRACTIONS

Fractions get their names from the digit on the bottom.
This apple is divided into 3 equal parts.
Each part is $\frac{1}{3}$ or **'one third'**

Here are some fractions and their names.

$\frac{1}{2}$	$\frac{1}{3}$	$\frac{1}{4}$	$\frac{1}{5}$	$\frac{1}{6}$	$\frac{1}{7}$	$\frac{1}{8}$	$\frac{1}{9}$	$\frac{1}{10}$
one half	one third	one quarter	one fifth	one sixth	one seventh	one eighth	one ninth	one tenth

Exercise 3

Copy and complete the sentences. The first one is done for you.

1. For 'one part of **three**' you say one third and you write $\frac{1}{3}$.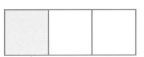

2. For 'one part of **five**' you say one fifth and you write . . .

3. For 'one part of **two**' you say . . . . and you write $\frac{1}{2}$

4. For 'one part of **six**' you say . . . . and you write . . .

5. For 'one part of **nine**' you say . . . . and you write . . .

6. For 'one part of **eight**' you say . . . . and you write . . .

7. For 'one part of **four**' you say . . . . and you write . . .

8. For 'one part of **ten**' you say . . . . and you write . . .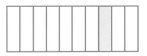

9. How many parts has a cake been divided into, if it has
    been cut into **a** tenths **b** quarters?

10. Six people will need a cake cut into . . . . equal parts,
    each part is called . . . . or . . . .

Example 1

The shape is divided into 4 parts.
One part is coloured.
$\frac{1}{4}$ of the shape is coloured.

Exercise 4

Answer these three questions for each drawing below.
a How many parts are there in the shape?
b How many parts are coloured?
c What fraction of the whole shape is coloured?

The first one is done for you.

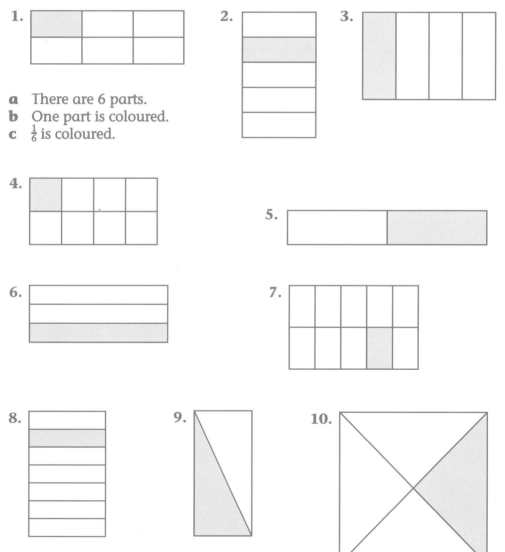

1.

a There are 6 parts.
b One part is coloured.
c $\frac{1}{6}$ is coloured.

2.

3.

4.

5.

6.

7.

8.

9.

10.

Exercise 5

Match the coloured part of each shape to the correct fraction.
If you think shape **1** is $\frac{1}{2}$, you write 1C.

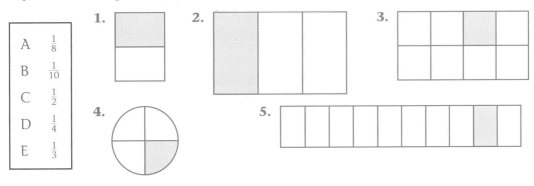

A	$\frac{1}{8}$
B	$\frac{1}{10}$
C	$\frac{1}{2}$
D	$\frac{1}{4}$
E	$\frac{1}{3}$

Exercise 6

Match the coloured part of each shape to the correct fraction.

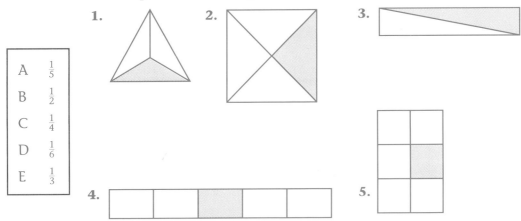

A	$\frac{1}{5}$
B	$\frac{1}{2}$
C	$\frac{1}{4}$
D	$\frac{1}{6}$
E	$\frac{1}{3}$

Exercise 7

Match the coloured part of each shape to the correct fraction.

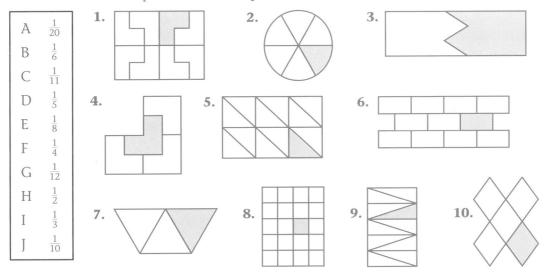

A	$\frac{1}{20}$
B	$\frac{1}{6}$
C	$\frac{1}{11}$
D	$\frac{1}{5}$
E	$\frac{1}{8}$
F	$\frac{1}{4}$
G	$\frac{1}{12}$
H	$\frac{1}{2}$
I	$\frac{1}{3}$
J	$\frac{1}{10}$

How Many Parts?

The top digit of a fraction shows how many parts you have.

This apple has been divided into 3 equal parts. Each part is $\frac{1}{3}$.
Two of the pieces have been taken away: $\frac{2}{3}$.
You say **'two thirds'** has been taken away.

A cake is divided into 4 equal parts, each part is $\frac{1}{4}$.
3 parts is called $\frac{3}{4}$.
You say **'three quarters'**.

Exercise 8

Copy and complete the sentences. The first one is done for you.

1. For **'two** parts of **three'** you say two thirds and you write $\frac{2}{3}$

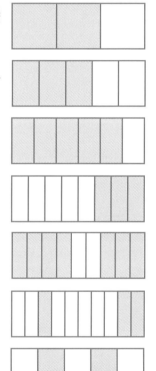

2. For **'three** parts of **five'** you say . . . . and you write . . .

3. For **'five** parts of **six'** you say . . . . and you write . . .

4. For **'three** parts of **eight'** you say . . . . and you write . . .

5. For **'seven** parts of **nine'** you say . . . . and you write . . .

6. For **'three** parts of **ten'** you say . . . . and you write . . .

7. For **'two** parts of **five'** you say . . . . and you write . . .

8. For **'nine** parts of **ten'** you say . . . . and you write . . .

9. What fraction of a cake is left, if **three quarters** of the cake is eaten?

10. Five friends share a 'mega pizza'. Two of the friends hate mushrooms and they scrape them off. What fraction of the pizza still has mushrooms. Write your answer in words as well as digits.

Example 2

The shape is divided into 3 parts.
Each part is $\frac{1}{3}$ of the whole shape.
2 parts are coloured so $\frac{2}{3}$ of the whole shape is coloured.

Exercise 9

Answer these three questions for each drawing.

a How many parts are there altogether?
b What fraction is each part of the whole shape?
c What fraction is coloured?

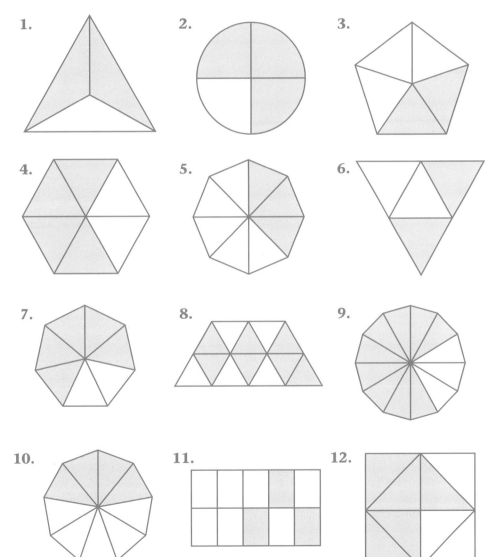

EQUAL SHARES

Steve and Roger are now sharing 8 sweets.
Steve shares them into two groups but as you can see the groups are not equal.

The shares are not fair .... So!

Exercise 10

1. Which drawing shows 10 mints shared into $\frac{1}{2}$s?

2. Which drawing shows 9 humbugs shared into $\frac{1}{3}$s?

3. Which drawing shows 12 toffees shared into $\frac{1}{4}$s?

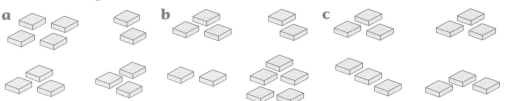

4. If these sweets are shared in $\frac{1}{2}$s, how many sweets will be in each group?

5. If these sweets are shared in $\frac{1}{3}$s, how many sweets will be in each group?

6. If these sweets are shared in $\frac{1}{4}$s, how many sweets will be in each group?

7. If these sweets are shared in $\frac{1}{2}$s, how many sweets will be in each group?

FRACTIONS OF AN AMOUNT

4 friends are going to share 8 cakes.
They will each get $\frac{1}{4}$ of the cakes.

$\frac{1}{4}$ of 8 cakes is 2, so each person will get 2 cakes.

Exercise 11

Copy and complete the table.

Number of people	Fraction each person will receive	Number of cakes to be shared	Number of cakes each person will receive
3	$\frac{1}{3}$	6	2
4	$\frac{1}{4}$	12	3
2		8	
3		9	
2		10	
4		8	
3		15	
5		15	
4		16	
3		12	

EQUAL FRACTIONS

Example 3

The cake has been cut into **quarters**, ($\frac{1}{4}$s)

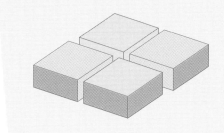

Two of the quarters is the same amount of cake as a half. $\frac{2}{4}$ is the same amount of cake as $\frac{1}{2}$.

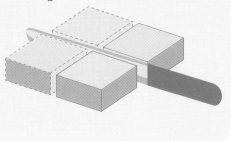

Exercise 12

Use the drawings below to decide if the two fractions are equal.

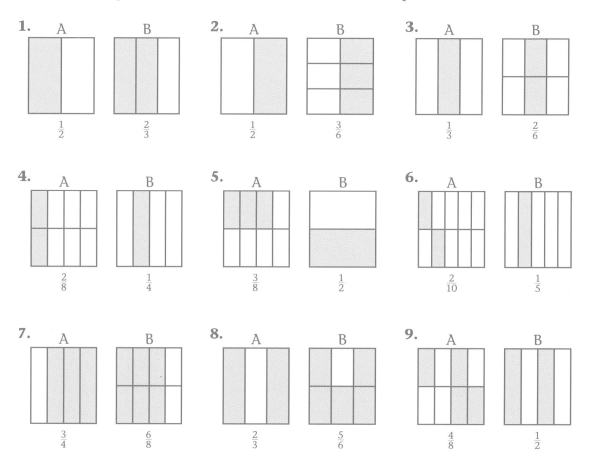

1. A   B
    $\frac{1}{2}$ $\frac{2}{3}$

2. A   B
    $\frac{1}{2}$ $\frac{3}{6}$

3. A   B
    $\frac{1}{3}$ $\frac{2}{6}$

4. A   B
    $\frac{2}{8}$ $\frac{1}{4}$

5. A   B
    $\frac{3}{8}$ $\frac{1}{2}$

6. A   B
    $\frac{2}{10}$ $\frac{1}{5}$

7. A   B
    $\frac{3}{4}$ $\frac{6}{8}$

8. A   B
    $\frac{2}{3}$ $\frac{5}{6}$

9. A   B
    $\frac{4}{8}$ $\frac{1}{2}$

Example 4

The beads have been divided into . . . halves ($\frac{1}{2}$s) . . . and then quarters ($\frac{1}{4}$s)

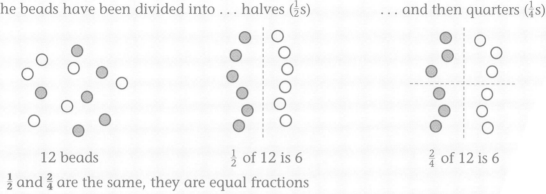

12 beads $\frac{1}{2}$ of 12 is 6 $\frac{2}{4}$ of 12 is 6

$\frac{1}{2}$ and $\frac{2}{4}$ are the same, they are equal fractions

Exercise 13

Decide whether these two fractions are equal. Write Equal or Not equal.
Use counters if it will help.

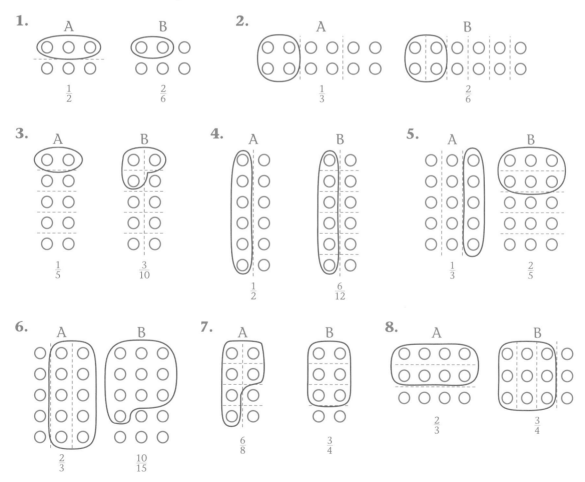

2 HOW MUCH DO YOU KNOW?

This unit will test how much you know, using 100 questions.

A. NUMBER WORK

Addition
1. 27 + 36 =
2. 144 + 217 =
3. 109 + 238 =
4. 337 + 288 =
5. 398 + 405 =
6. 226 + 989 =

Subtraction
7. 68 − 35 =
8. 87 − 34 =
9. 80 − 27 =
10. 360 − 157 =
11. 415 − 145 =
12. 652 − 146 =

Multiplication
13. 4 × 2 =
14. 3 × 5 =
15. 4 × 4 =
16. 7 × 4 =
17. 2 × 9 =
18. 8 × 3 =

Division
19. 6 ÷ 2 =
20. 9 ÷ 3 =
21. 10 ÷ 2 =
22. 12 ÷ 2 =
23. 25 ÷ 5 =
24. 24 ÷ 4 =

B. PERIMETER

What is the perimeter of each shape?
The drawings are not to scale.

25.

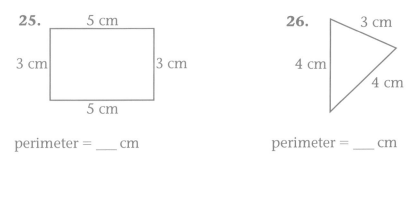

5 cm
3 cm   3 cm
5 cm

perimeter = ___ cm

26.

3 cm
4 cm
4 cm

perimeter = ___ cm

27.

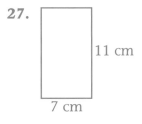

11 cm
7 cm

perimeter = ___ cm

28.

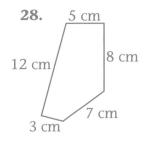

5 cm
12 cm   8 cm
3 cm   7 cm

perimeter = ___ cm

C.   FRACTIONS

What fraction of each shape is shaded?

29.

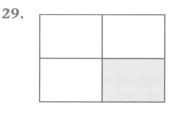

30.

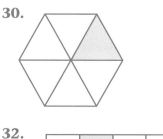

31.

32.

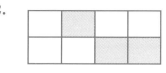

D.   PATTERNS IN NUMBER

Copy and complete these numbers patterns.

33. 10, 15, __, 25, __   **34.** 5, 9, 13, 17, __, __
35. 6, 10, __, 18, __, 26   **36.** 2, 5, 8, 11, __, __
37. 30, 27, 24, 21, __, __   **38.** 28, 25, 22, __, __, 13
39. 90, __, 70, 60, 50, __   **40.** 30, 25, 20, __, __, 5

E.   MONEY

Complete these sums.

41. £ : p	**42.** £ : p	**43.** £ : p	**44.** £ : p	**45.** £ : p
3 18	4 27	12 64	21 58	9 88
+ 5 21	+ 5 36	+ 34 94	+ 4 64	+ 37 27

Here are the prices of some products in a supermarket.

SOAP   29p

CHEESE   54p

BEANS   31p

46. How much would a tin of beans and a pack of butter cost?
47. How much would a bar of soap and a tin of beans cost?
48. How much would a tin of beans and a pack of cheese cost?
49. How much would a pack of cheese and a bar of soap cost?
50. How much would two tins of beans cost?
51. How much would two bars of soap cost?

BUTTER   50p

F.   TIME

Match the two clocks which show the same time.
Clock **52** shows the same time as clock C, so you write **52C**.

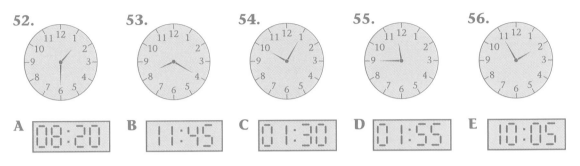

52.   **53.**   **54.**   **55.**   **56.**

A `08:20`   B `11:45`   C `01:30`   D `01:55`   E `10:05`

G.   ANGLES

What angles are shown on these protractors?

57.   **58.**

59.   **60.**

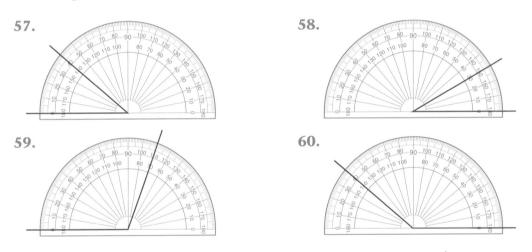

H.   PROBLEMS TO DO IN YOUR HEAD

61. Tom has 56p, Gill has 30p and Tim has 40p. How much have they in total?
62. If there are 11 sweets in a packet, how many sweets are in 3 packets?
63. There are 32 people in a room. If 6 people leave, how many are left?
64. Two children share 18p equally. How much does each get?
65. What is the total of £5, £4, £7 and 26p?
66. Mary has 97p. She spends 57p. How much has she left?
67. What is six times three?
68. How many times does 3 go into 15?
69. Add four to ninety-nine.
70. Take 222 from 555.

I. ALGEBRA

Copy these problems and write in the missing number.

71. $\square + 5 = 11$ **72.** $\square + 12 = 20$ **73.** $9 + \square = 21$

74. $12 - \square = 10$ **75.** $\square - 3 = 2$

What is the value of these expressions if
   w is worth 4
   x is worth 7
   y is worth 2
and z is worth 3?

76. $x + z = \square$ **77.** $z + y = \square$ **78.** $x + y = \square$

79. $w + x - z = \square$ **80.** $x + z + w - y = \square$

J. STATISTICS

What numbers are shown on these tallies?

81. 𝍸𝍸 || **82 .** 𝍸 𝍸 𝍸 ||| **83.** 𝍸 𝍸 𝍸 𝍸 ||| **84.** 𝍸 𝍸 𝍸 𝍸 𝍸

The bar chart shows the attendance of
six classes in one day.
Answer the questions about the bar chart.

85. Which class had the highest attendance?
86. Which class had the lowest attendance?
87. How many pupils in 8Y attended?
88. How many pupils in 8H attended?
89. How many pupils in 8B attended?
90. How many pupils in 8N attended?
91. How many pupils in 8C attended?
92. How many pupils in 8T attended?
93. Which classes had the same attendance?
94. Which class had 29 pupils attending?

K. SHAPES

Copy and complete these symmetrical letters to make a word.

95. BOXED

Draw the completed symmetrical shapes below.

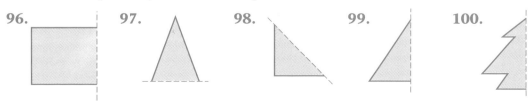

96.   **97.**   **98.**   **99.**   **100.**

3 WORKING WITH NUMBER

This unit will help you to:
→ **find different ways to multiply and divide.**

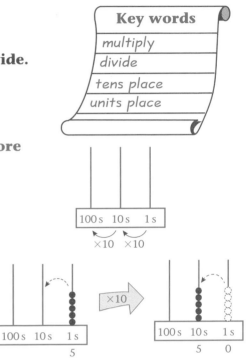

Key words

multiply
divide
tens place
units place

MULTIPLYING BY 10

Each spike on the abacus is worth **ten times more** than the spike to its right.

A bead on the 10 spike, is worth ten times more than a bead on the units (1s) spike.

To **multiply a number by 10** you just shift the beads along to the next spike or *place* to the left.

So to **multiply 5 by ten**, move the 5 beads from the units spike onto the tens spike.

The **5 tens** are worth **50**.

Another way of looking at multiplying by ten:

100s   10s   1s

5 × 10   move the 5 one place to the left.

5   0 ————— put a **0** into the **'units place'** because there are no units.

Exercise 1

Write down the numbers that are ten times bigger than these.

1. **a** 2   **b** 4   **c** 6   **d** 8
   e 7   **f** 5   **g** 3   **h** 9

2. Below are some multiplications that are wrong.
   Explain why they cannot be correct.
   a   43 × 10 = 431
   b   60 × 10 = 606
   c   50 × 10 = 5

Exercise 2

Solve these problems about multiplying by ten.

1. Each pipe is 10 m long. If they are all laid end-to-end, how far will they stretch?

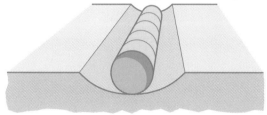

2. This drain is 80 m long. How many 10 m pipes will be needed?

3. Each bag of cement weighs 10 kg. The trolley can carry up to 100 kg. Can they all be carried in one journey?

4. How many coins will you get when you change £7 into 10p coins?

MULTIPLYING LARGER NUMBERS BY 10

To multiply 16 by 10, move all of the beads, one place to the left.

The single bead moves one place to the left to the **'hundreds'** spike.
The six beads move one place to the left, onto the **'tens'** spike.
There are no units so you write a **0** into the units place.

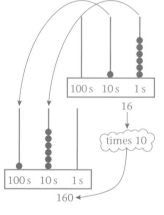

100s	10s	1s	
	1	6	× 10
1	6	**0**	

Exercise 3

Multiply these numbers by 10.

1. 13 × 10 =	**2.** 12 × 10 =	**3.** 17 × 10 =
4. 19 × 10 =	**5.** 32 × 10 =	**6.** 53 × 10 =
7. 47 × 10 =	**8.** 58 × 10 =	**9.** 51 × 10 =
10. 86 × 10 =	**11.** 20 × 10 =	**12.** 50 × 10 =

Exercise 4

Solve these problems by multiplying by ten.

1. A pipeline is made from small sections that are each 10 m long. How long will the pipeline be if it is made from 15 small sections?

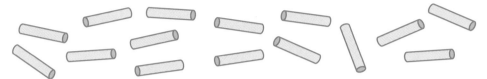

2. Eggs are packed in boxes of 10. How many eggs will you be able to pack into 18 boxes?

3. Mr Poole travels by car to work each day. In one day his car uses 10 litres of petrol. How many litres will it use in 30 days?

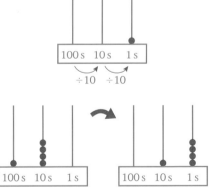

4. If you change £17.50 into 10p coins, how many coins will you have?

5. Every time that the larger wheel turns once, the smaller wheel turns 10 times.
   How many times will the smaller wheel turn if the large wheel turns 25 times?

DIVIDING BY TEN

Each spike on the abacus is worth **ten times less** than the spike on its left.

To **divide by ten** you can move the beads one place to the right.

So, 140 ÷ 10 = 14

↙ divided by

Another way to think of dividing by 10:

100s 10s   1s
  1   4   0   ÷ 10
        1   4

$$140 ÷ 10 = 14$$

Exercise 5

Divide these whole numbers by 10.

1. 70 ÷ 10 =	**2.** 90 ÷ 10 =	**3.** 10 ÷ 10 =	**4.** 100 ÷ 10 =
5. 110 ÷ 10 =	**6.** 500 ÷ 10 =	**7.** 170 ÷ 10 =	**8.** 200 ÷ 10 =
9. 700 ÷ 10 =	**10.** 900 ÷ 10 =	**11.** 840 ÷ 10 =	**12.** 1000 ÷ 10 =

Exercise 6

Use division or multiplication by 10 to solve these problems.

1. The length of a London bus is about 10 m.
How many buses will fit end-to-end across Hammersmith Bridge?

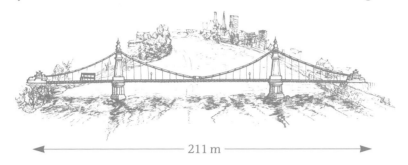

— 211 m —

2. A lift can take 10 people. If there are 82 people waiting to use the lift, how many trips will it have to make to carry everyone?

3. The window has 10 panes of glass.
How many panes will be needed for 22 windows?

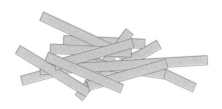

4. The fence section below is made from 10 pieces of timber.
How many fence sections can be made from 111 pieces of timber?

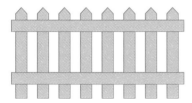

DOUBLE AND TREBLING ....

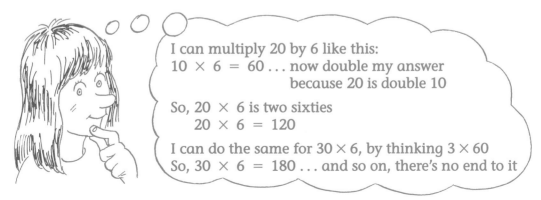

I can multiply 20 by 6 like this:
$10 \times 6 = 60$ ... now double my answer
because 20 is double 10

So, 20×6 is two sixties
$20 \times 6 = 120$

I can do the same for 30×6, by thinking 3×60
So, $30 \times 6 = 180$ ... and so on, there's no end to it

Exercise 7

Copy and complete these questions. When you feel confident, you can just answer part **b**.

1. **a** $10 \times 7 =$ **b** $20 \times 7 =$ remember that (20 is **2** $\times$ 10)
2. **a** $10 \times 5 =$ **b** $30 \times 5 =$ remember that (30 is **3** $\times$ 10)
3. **a** $10 \times 3 =$ **b** $30 \times 3 =$ remember that (30 is **3** $\times$ 10)
4. **a** $10 \times 4 =$ **b** $40 \times 4 =$ remember that (40 is **4** $\times$ 10)
5. **a** $10 \times 8 =$ **b** $30 \times 8 =$ remember that (30 is **3** $\times$ 10)
6. **a** $10 \times 6 =$ **b** $30 \times 6 =$ remember that (30 is **3** $\times$ 10)
7. **a** $10 \times 4 =$ **b** $50 \times 4 =$ remember that (50 is **5** $\times$ 10)
8. **a** $10 \times 5 =$ **b** $60 \times 5 =$ remember that (60 is **6** $\times$ 10)
9. **a** $10 \times 4 =$ **b** $70 \times 4 =$ remember that (70 is **7** $\times$ 10)
10. **a** $10 \times 9 =$ **b** $20 \times 9 =$ remember that (20 is **2** $\times$ 10)

Exercise 8

Solve these problems using your multiplication skills.

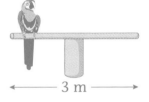

1. Polly parrot can walk 3 m to the right and then 3 m back again.
   a How far does Polly walk if she travels from one end of her perch to the other and back again?
   b If she walks from one end to the other and back again ten times, how far will she travel altogether?
   c Polly makes 30 trips back and forwards. How far does she walk altogether?

   ← 3 m →

2. **a** This is a piece of elastic, measure it.

   Complete this sentence. 'The elastic is . . . cm long.'
   b If the elastic was stretched to be **10 times** longer, how long would it be?
   c The elastic will snap when it is stretched past 230 cm. Now imagine that the elastic is stretched to make it **30 times** longer. Will it snap? Say how you know.

3. Zayd has saved £4, Emmanuel has saved £120.
   Say which of these statements is true:
   a Emmanuel has saved 10 times more than Zayd.
   b Emmanuel has saved 30 times more than Zayd.
   c Zayd has saved 40 times more than Emmanuel.

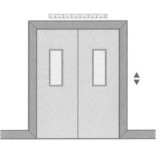

4. The lift travels 3 m between each floor.
   How far does it travel if it goes up:
   a   10 floors
   b   5 floors
   c   35 floors?

USING TEN TO DIVIDE BY 20, 30 ...

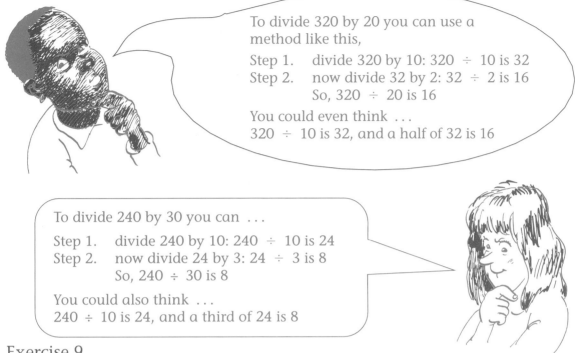

To divide 320 by 20 you can use a method like this,

Step 1.   divide 320 by 10: 320 ÷ 10 is 32
Step 2.   now divide 32 by 2: 32 ÷ 2 is 16
            So, 320 ÷ 20 is 16

You could even think . . .
320 ÷ 10 is 32, and a half of 32 is 16

To divide 240 by 30 you can . . .

Step 1.   divide 240 by 10: 240 ÷ 10 is 24
Step 2.   now divide 24 by 3: 24 ÷ 3 is 8
            So, 240 ÷ 30 is 8

You could also think . . .
240 ÷ 10 is 24, and a third of 24 is 8

Exercise 9

Divide these numbers. If you need help you can answer parts **b** and **c** before part **a**.

1. **a** 270 ÷ 30 =   (**b** 270 ÷ 10 =   **c** 27 ÷ 3 =)
2. **a** 350 ÷ 50 =   (**b** 350 ÷ 10 =   **c** 35 ÷ 5 =)
3. **a** 180 ÷ 20 =   (**b** 180 ÷ 10 =   **c** 18 ÷ 2 =)
4. **a** 140 ÷ 20 =   (**b** 140 ÷ 10 =   **c** 14 ÷ 2 =)
5. **a** 280 ÷ 40 =   (**b** 280 ÷ 10 =   **c** 28 ÷ 4 =)
6. **a** 400 ÷ 50 =   (**b** 400 ÷ 10 =   **c** 40 ÷ 5 =)
7. **a** 360 ÷ 40 =   (**b** 360 ÷ 10 =   **c** 36 ÷ 4 =)
8. **a** 450 ÷ 50 =   (**b** 450 ÷ 10 =   **c** 45 ÷ 5 =)
9. **a** 320 ÷ 80 =   (**b** 320 ÷ 10 =   **c** 32 ÷ 8 =)
10. **a** 500 ÷ 50 =   (**b** 500 ÷ 10 =   **c** 50 ÷ 5 =)

Exercise 10

This is the picture of an ant magnified to 20 times its real length.
How long is the ant in real life?

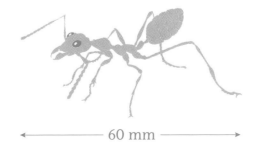

←——— 60 mm ———→

4 TIME

This unit will help you to:
→ **understand a.m., p.m., and 24-hour times**
→ **calculate passing time**
→ **use a timetable and units of time.**

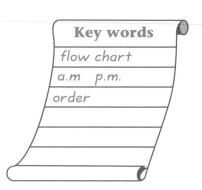

Key words
flow chart
a.m   p.m.
order

GETTING THINGS IN THE RIGHT ORDER

Exercise 1

Look at the 'Crazy Alarm Clock'. Copy and complete the 'flow chart' below it to explain how it works.

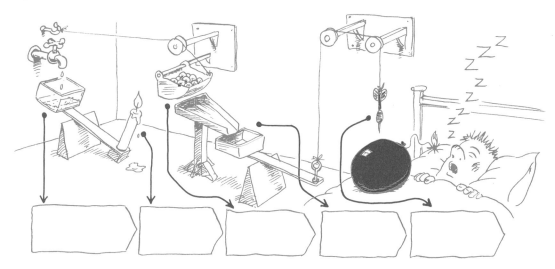

Exercise 2

Making a hot dog. Put the 'flow chart' instructions in order to produce a hot dog.

a PLACE ONIONS ON HOT DOG

b LAY NAPKIN ON TABLE

c CUT THE ROLL

d POUR SAUCE OVER ONIONS

e PLACE ROLL ON NAPKINS

f PLACE HOT DOG ON ROLL

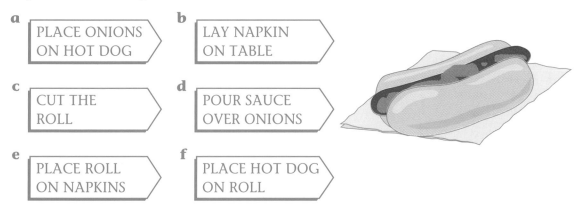

Exercise 3

Here are nine steps to make a pancake.
Draw a 'flow chart' to describe the steps. The first is done for you.

1. You need oil, milk, flour, sugar and eggs
2.
3.
4.
5.
6.
7.
8.
9.

Exercise 4

This is Mrs Shaw's Safety Firework Lighter.

1. Draw a 'flow chart' to explain how the Firework Lighter works.
2. In what ways could weather (wind, fog, rain) affect how well it works?

NUMERACY MEASURING TIME

You can measure time in these units:

seconds   minutes   hours   days   months   years

You must choose the most sensible unit.

Here are some crazy records. Note the different units used for each record.

The world record for eating 91 pickled onions is 68 seconds.

M. Lotito ate a bicycle in 15 days.

Mr Anadan balanced on one leg for 33 hours.

Jay Gwaltney ate a tree trunk 3.35 m long in 3 days 17 hours.

The world's oldest living tree is over 6000 years

Exercise 5

Which unit would you use to measure these lengths of time?

1. How long you sleep each night.
2. The time taken to tie your shoe laces.
3. The time taken to write your name.
4. The time taken to travel to school.
5. How long it is until Sunday.
6. The time taken to eat a bag of crisps.
7. The time taken to clap 15 times.
8. The time taken to brush your teeth.

Clocks and calendars are used to record or to measure time.

Exercise 6

Copy and complete these sentences.

1. There are ____ minutes in an hour.
2. There are ____ days in a week.
3. There are ____ months in a year.
4. There are ____ seconds in a minute.

Use **longer** or **shorter** to complete these sentences:

5. An hour is _____ than a minute.
6. A month is _____ than a year.
7. A minute is _____ than a second.
8. A month is _____ than a week.

MINUTES

Exercise 7

1. Rupert took part in a car rally.
Clock A shows the time when he started.
Clock B shows the time when he finished.
How many minutes did he take?

Clock A   Clock B

2. Miranda went to her science lesson.
Clock A shows when the lesson began.
Clock B shows when the lesson finished.
How many minutes have passed?

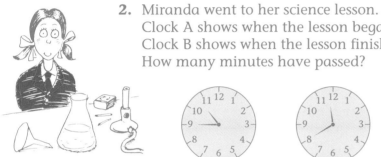

Clock A   Clock B

How many minutes have passed between the times shown?

3.   **4.**   **5.**

6.   **7.**   **8.**

Exercise 8

1. Tom left for school at 8 o'clock. He arrived at 20 minutes past 8.
How long did it take him?
2. Mary started her exercises at '10 past 4' and finished at '25 past 4'.
How long was she doing her exercises?
3. Mum started making tea at '10 to 4' and finished at '15 minutes past 4'.
How long did it take her to make tea?
4. Dad started washing the windows at 3 o'clock and finished at '10 to 4'.
How long did it take him to wash the windows?

This clock says
'30 minutes past 4'
or 'half past 4'.

 This clock says
'quarter to 4'.

This clock says
'quarter past 4'.

Exercise 9

Copy and complete these sentences.

1. This clock shows a quarter past 6.
   This is the same as ____ minutes past 6.

2. This clock shows a quarter to 4.
   This is the same as ____ minutes to 4.

3. This clock shows half past 10.
   This is the same as ____ minutes past 10.

4. This clock shows 2.45.
   This is the same as quarter to ____.

5. This clock shows 6.45.
   This is the same as ____ minutes to 7.

Exercise 10

Write down how many minutes pass between:

1. 6 o'clock and half past 6
2. 9 o'clock and quarter past 9
3. 2 o'clock and quarter to 3
4. half past 9 and 10 o'clock
5. quarter to 7 and 7 o'clock
6. quarter to 5 and quarter past 5
7. half past 6 and 7 o'clock
8. quarter to 10 and quarter past 10
9. quarter past 2 and quarter to 3
10. half past 8 and quarter to 9

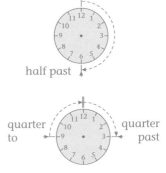

half past

quarter
to

quarter
past

HOURS AND MINUTES

Exercise 11

1. Cathy left for work at 7 o'clock.
She got to work at 20 minutes past 8.
How many hours and minutes did her journey take?

2. Robert starts playing football at 3 o'clock.
He finishes at half past 4.
How many hours and minutes does the game last?

3. Mary drove to her friend's house in York.
She left at 8 o'clock and arrived at half past 9.
How many hours and minutes did the journey take?

Exercise 12

Mick took part in a marathon. During the race, he saw a number of clocks.
The race started at 2 o'clock.
Write down how long had he been running when he saw:

1. the Town Hall clock
2. the clock in the square
3. the Station clock
4. the Market clock
5. the clock at the finish.

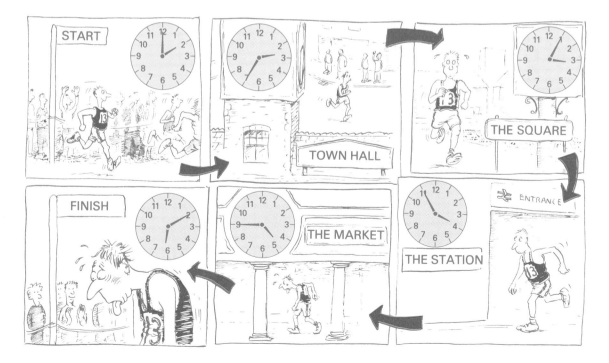

DAYS

To record days, weeks and months,
you use a calendar.
Here is a calendar showing the
month of October.

October					
Sunday		6	13	20	27
Monday		7	14	21	28
Tuesday	1	8 ✓	15	22	29
Wednesday	2	9	16	23	30
Thursday	3	10	17 ✗	24	31
Friday	4	11	18	25	
Saturday	5	12	19	26	

Exercise 13

Look at the calendar, then answer the questions below.

1. How many days are there in October?

2. On which day does October begin?

3. On which day will 23rd October fall?

4. What date will it be on the last Tuesday of the month?

5. On which day does October end?

6. What will be the date on the first Thursday of the month?

7. On which day will 16th October fall?

8. On which day will 8th October fall?

9. What is the date marked with a ✗?

10. What is the date marked with a ✓?

Exercise 14

Use the calendar above to answer these questions.

1. Tom begins his holiday on Thursday 10th October. The last day of his holiday is Sunday 20th October. How long is the holiday?

2. The first day of Anne's school journey is marked with a ✓ and the last day with a ✗. How many days does the journey last?

3 Jenny's exams begin on Monday 21st October and end on Thursday 24th October. How many days do the exams last?

4. Bob's holidays begins on Monday 14th October. He has 9 days holiday. What is the date of the last day of his holiday?

5. Mandy's holiday begins on Wednesday 2nd October. She has 14 days holiday. What is the date of the last day of her holiday?

6. a How many Sundays are there in this month?
   b How many Tuesdays are there in this month?
   c How many Fridays are there in this month?

THE 24-HOUR CLOCK

Captain Bulldog wants to see his soldiers at 7 o'clock, but the soldiers are confused.

Does he mean 7 o'clock in the morning or 7 o'clock at night?

To clear up the confusion, the captain repeats the order using the 24-hour clock.

He says he wants to see the soldiers at 19.00 hours.

A day begins a moment after 12 o'clock midnight, and lasts for the next 24 hours. The hour hand of a clock travels around the clock face twice a day. So 7 o'clock will appear twice in a day.

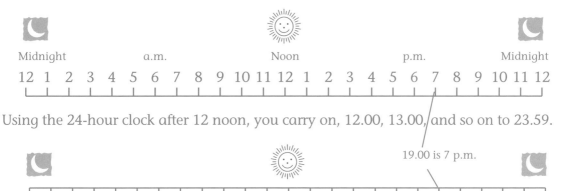

Using the 24-hour clock after 12 noon, you carry on, 12.00, 13.00, and so on to 23.59.

19.00 is 7 p.m.

00.00 01.00 02.00 03.00 04.00 05.00 06.00 07.00 08.00 09.00 10.00 11.00 12.00 13.00 14.00 15.00 16.00 17.00 18.00 19.00 20.00 21.00 22.00 23.00 00.00

Exercise 15

Using this time diagram, copy and complete the sentences below.

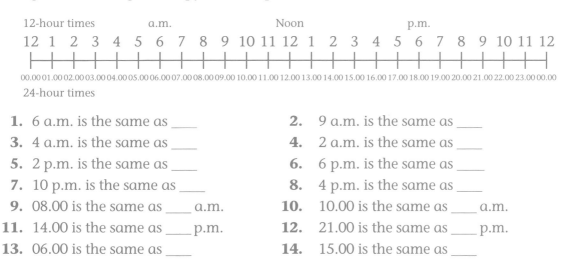

1. 6 a.m. is the same as ____
2. 9 a.m. is the same as ____
3. 4 a.m. is the same as ____
4. 2 a.m. is the same as ____
5. 2 p.m. is the same as ____
6. 6 p.m. is the same as ____
7. 10 p.m. is the same as ____
8. 4 p.m. is the same as ____
9. 08.00 is the same as ____ a.m.
10. 10.00 is the same as ____ a.m.
11. 14.00 is the same as ____ p.m.
12. 21.00 is the same as ____ p.m.
13. 06.00 is the same as ____
14. 15.00 is the same as ____

It is 8:30 in the morning.   It is 2:15 in the afternoon.

The 12-hour clock shows 8.30 a.m.   The 12-hour clock shows 2.15 p.m.
The 24-hour clock shows 08.30.   The 24-hour clock shows 14.15.

With the 24-hour clock, you do not need to use a.m. or p.m.

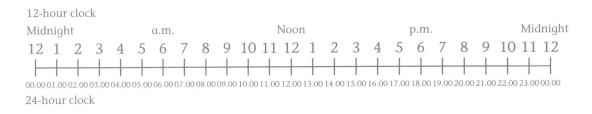

Exercise 16

Write each time as a 24-hour clock time.

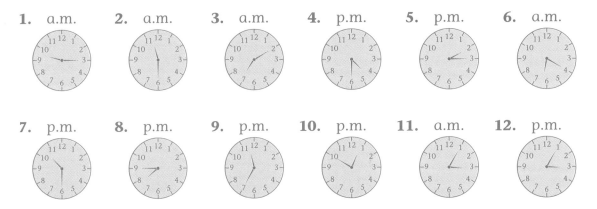

1. a.m.   2. a.m.   3. a.m.   4. p.m.   5. p.m.   6. a.m.

7. p.m.   8. p.m.   9. p.m.   10. p.m.   11. a.m.   12. p.m.

Exercise 17

Write these 24-hour clock times as 12-hour clock times. Remember to put in whether
the time is a.m. or p.m.

1. 05.30	**2.** 07.15	**3.** 13.30	**4.** 18.00
5. 09.20	**6.** 16.45	**7.** 04.20	**8.** 11.25
9. 19.30	**10.** 22.10	**11.** 10.10	**12.** 23.50

TIMETABLES

Most travel timetables use the 24-hour clock.

Exercise 18

Here is a timetable for a Scottish ferry.

Mallaig	10.30 hrs
Eigg	12.00 hrs
Rhum	13.30 hrs
Canna	14.45 hrs

Use the timetable to answer the questions.
1. Where does the ferry stop at 12 noon?
2. Where does the ferry stop at 1.30 p.m.?
3. How long does it take the ferry to get from Mallaig to Rhum?
4. Between which two islands will the ferry be at 2 p.m.?
5. How long does the journey take from Mallaig to Canna?

Exercise 19

Three trains a day travel from Kyle of Lochalsh to Inverness.

	First train	Second train	Third train
Kyle of Lochalsh	07.10	11.50	17.05
Plockton	07.25	12.05	17.20
Stromeferry	07.35	12.15	17.30
Strathcarron	07.53	12.32	17.50
Achnasheen	08.21	13.00	18.15
Garve	08.45	13.28	18.50
Dingwall	09.15	13.55	19.10
Muir of Ord	09.25	14.00	19.20
Inverness	09.40	14.25	19.40

Use the timetable to answer the questions.
1. What times does the first train leave Kyle of Lochalsh in the morning?
2. Does the first train arrive in Inverness at 9.40 a.m. or 9.40 p.m.?
3. Where is the first train at 8.45 a.m.?
4. Where is the second train at 1.00 p.m.?
5. Where is the third train at 6.50 p.m.?
6. Where is the third train at 7.40 p.m.?
7. How long does the third train take to get from Plockton to Garve?
8. Does each journey from Kyle of Lochalsh to Inverness take more than 3 hours or less than 3 hours?
9. You arrive at Plockton at 11 a.m. What time is the next train?
10. You arrive at Garve at 5.30 p.m. What time is the next train?

YEARS

Our planet Earth was formed many, many millions of years ago.
However, our calendar does not start at this point.
A moment in history was chosen; around the time of the birth of Christ.
Time before the birth of Christ is described as BC (Before Christ).
Time after the birth of Christ is described as AD (Anno Domini).

Exercise 20

Use the timeline below to answer the questions.

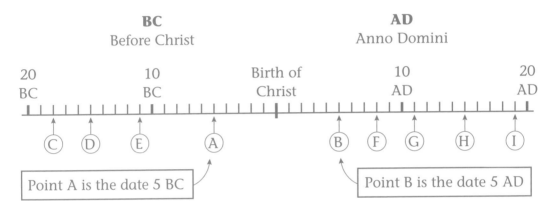

The difference between point A and point B is 10 years.

1. What dates are shown at the following points – remember to use BC or AD.
   a F   **b** D   **c** H   **d** C   **e** E   **f** I
2. How many years are shown on the time line?
3. How many years are there between point B and G?
4. How many years are there between point A and F?
5. How many years are there between point E and B?
6. How many years are there between point D and B?
7. How many years are there between point E and H?
8. How many years are there between point C and I?

Exercise 21

1. Copy the time line and fill in the missing dates.

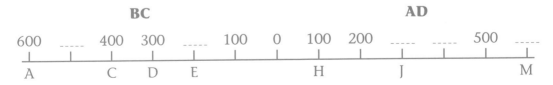

2. How many hundreds of years difference are there between:
   a A and E   **b** E and H   **c** D and J   **d** C and M?

Exercise 22

Where do these events belong on the timeline?
If you think event 3 should be at point F on the timeline, write **3F**.

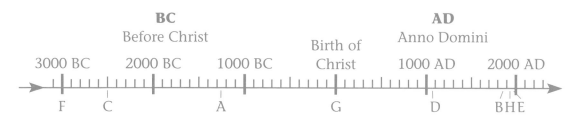

1. The invention of the first car.
   1885 AD

2. The building of the Great Pyramid.
   2500 BC

3. The earliest form of writing.
   3000 BC

4. The birth of Christ.

5. The Battle of Hastings.
   1066 AD

6. The year of your birth.
   ?

7. The first man goes into space.
   1961 AD

8. The Trojan War.
   1250 BC

9. How many years are shown on the timeline?
10. How many years are there between 1000 BC and 1000 AD?
11. How many years are there between 2000 BC and 2000 AD?
12 How many years are there between 3000 BC and 1000 AD?

5 CONGRUENCE

Key words

congruent

triangle

square

tessellate

hexagon

This unit will help you to:
→ **understand the word congruent**
→ **find congruent shapes**
→ **understand the word tessellation and tessellate shapes.**

FITTING SHAPES

Exercise 1

Decide which jigsaw piece will fit the spaces below. There is only one correct piece for each drawing.

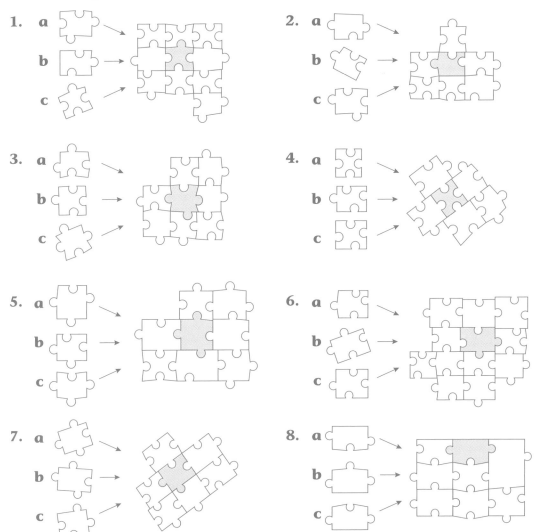

CONGRUENT SHAPES

Shapes which are exactly the same size and shape are **congruent**.

Example 1

These drawings may look the same, but only two are **exactly** the same size and shape.

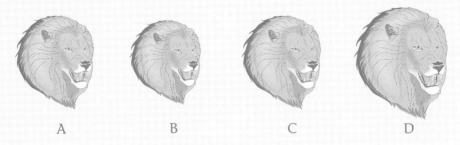

Drawings **A** and **C** are **congruent**.
They are exactly the same shape and size. You can trace the outline of each shape to check.

Exercise 2

In each question find which shapes are congruent to shape **a**. Use tracing paper to help you decide.

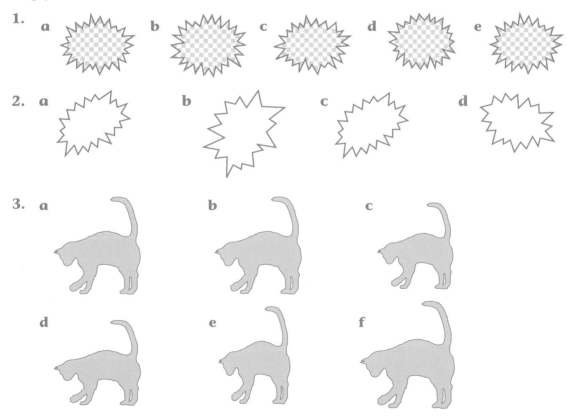

Measuring for congruence

You can measure shapes and compare them to see if they are congruent.

Example 2

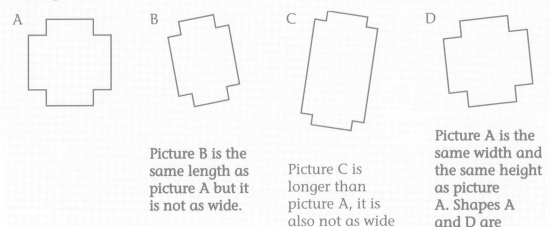

Picture B is the same length as picture A but it is not as wide.

Picture C is longer than picture A, it is also not as wide as picture A.

Picture A is the same width and the same height as picture A. Shapes A and D are **congruent**.

Exercise 3

There are two congruent shapes in each question. Measure all the shapes and compare them to find the congruent shapes.

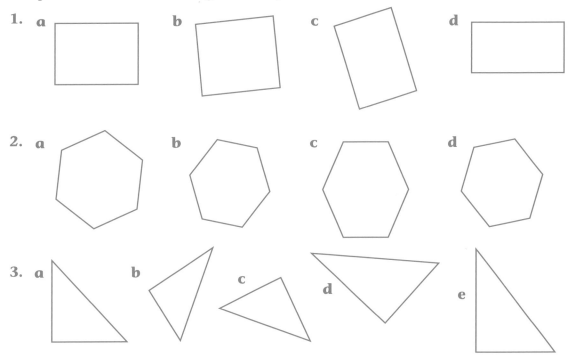

GROWING SHAPE PATTERNS

Exercise 4

The smaller triangle has been used to build the pattern for the larger triangle.

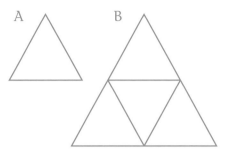

1. Trace the triangle patterns into your book.
2. Use tracing paper to make the next triangle in the pattern.
3. How many triangles make up:
   a the first pattern
   b the second pattern
   c the third pattern?

Exercise 5

Here is another 'growing' pattern using squares.

1. Trace or draw the square patterns into your book.
2. Draw the next two square patterns.

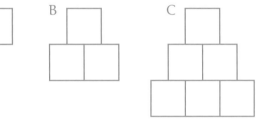

3. How many squares make up:
   a the first square pattern
   b the second square pattern
   c the third square pattern
   d the fourth square pattern
   e the fifth square pattern?

Exercise 6

Trace these two shapes. Draw the hexagon into your book.

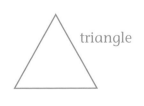

triangle

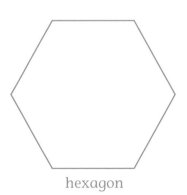

hexagon

1. Fill the hexagon with triangles.
2. How many triangles filled the hexagon?

Exercise 7

Trace these 'L' shapes.

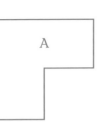

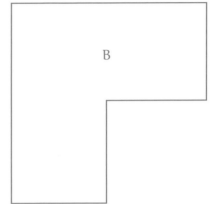

1. Fit as many of shape A into
    shape B as you can. There should
    be no gaps or overlaps.
2. How many shapes like A are needed
    to make shape B?

TESSELLATIONS

A tessellation is a pattern which is made by repeating a shape over and over again.
The pattern must have no gaps and no other shapes in it.

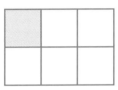

This is a tessellation made from
square tiles.

Tiles can be arranged in any direction
as long as no gaps are left.

Exercise 8

Which of these tiling patterns are tessellations of the shaded shape?

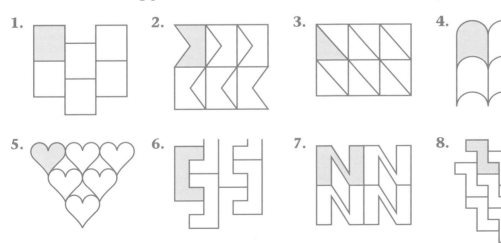

This drawing is made by tessellating the lizard shape.

The drawing was made by M.C. Escher.

Exercise 9

Some of the shapes below will tessellate, some will not. Decide on a way to test them. Make tessellation patterns from the shapes that will tessellate.

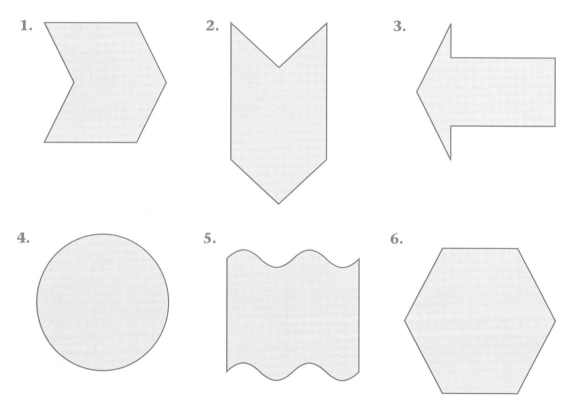

1.

2.

3.

4.

5.

6.

 6 THE FOUR RULES 1

Key words

addition (+)
subtraction (−)
multiplication (×)
times (×)
division (÷)
share (÷)

This unit will help you to:
→ **read and write numbers**
→ **work out calculations in your head**
→ **practice addition, subtraction, multiplication and division.**

ADDITION (+)

Work these sums out in your head.
Spend 10 minutes on each card; see how many you can complete.

Addition workcard 1	
1. 23 + 14 =	**2.** 46 + 23 =
3. 22 + 57 =	**4.** 36 + 10 =
5. 54 + 20 =	**6.** 20 + 47 =
7. 26 + 16 =	**8.** 37 + 36 =
9. 45 + 27 =	**10.** 38 + 35 =

Addition workcard 2	
1. 56 + 27 =	**2.** 24 + 28 =
3. 36 + 26 =	**4.** 48 + 28 =
5. 19 + 37 =	**6.** 57 + 28 =
7. 36 + 39 =	**8.** 43 + 48 =
9. 57 + 37 =	**10.** 66 + 18 =

Exercise 1

1. 625 There is a ___ in the 100s column.

2. 252 There is a ___ in the 10s column.

3. 518 There is a ___ in the 1s column.

4. 105 There is a ___ in the 10s column.

5. 353 There is a ___ in the 100s column.

6. 283 There is a ___ in the 1s column.

7. What does **6** stand for in 326 ?

8. What does **3** stand for in 532 ?

9. What does **2** stand for in 215 ?

10. What does **8** stand for in 380 ?

11. What does **4** stand for in 493 ?

12. What does **3** stand for in 513 ?

Addition workcard 3	
1. 18 + 12 =	**2.** 35 + 25 =
3. 41 + 19 =	**4.** 54 + 36 =
5. 27 + 23 =	**6.** 16 + 24 =
7. 25 + 29 =	**8.** 46 + 47 =
9. 38 + 32 =	**10.** 16 + 49 =

Addition workcard 4	
1. 125 + 253 =	**2.** 214 + 375 =
3. 443 + 456 =	**4.** 256 + 116 =
5. 347 + 224 =	**6.** 559 + 315 =
7. 260 + 253 =	**8.** 167 + 190 =
9. 371 + 154 =	**10.** 256 + 250 =

SUBTRACTION (−)

Work these subtraction sums out in your head.
Spend 10 minutes on each workcard; see how many you can complete.

Subtraction workcard 1	
1. 9 − 6 =	**2.** 12 − 8 =
3. 10 − 3 =	**4.** 15 − 9 =
5. 17 − 8 =	**6.** 20 − 13 =
7. 21 − 11 =	**8.** 23 − 17 =
9. 22 − 15 =	**10.** 21 − 16 =

Subtraction workcard 2	
1. 21 − 19 =	**2.** 33 − 26 =
3. 24 − 15 =	**4.** 25 − 7 =
5. 32 − 6 =	**6.** 37 − 8 =
7. 25 − 10 =	**8.** 45 − 20 =
9. 45 − 8 =	**10.** 26 − 10 =

Exercise 2

1. Take one from 100.

2. Take 90 from 100.

3. Take 5 from 50.

4. Take one from 200.

5. Take 10 from 100.

6. Take 10 from 300.

7. Take 50 from 600.

8. Take 5 from 200.

9. What is the difference between 30 and 50?

10. What is the difference between 20 and 45?

11. What is the difference between 40 and 75?

12. What is the difference between 30 and 85?

13. What is the difference between 20 and 47?

14. What is the difference between 40 and 73?

Subtraction workcard 3	
1. 35 − 25 =	**2.** 41 − 19 =
3. 80 − 43 =	**4.** 65 − 28 =
5. 53 − 28 =	**6.** 71 − 53 =
7. 62 − 47 =	**8.** 73 − 17 =
9. 50 − 34 =	**10.** 51 − 16 =

Subtraction workcard 4	
1. 428 − 213 =	**2.** 649 − 125 =
3. 124 − 113 =	**4.** 884 − 323 =
5. 388 − 265 =	**6.** 370 − 227 =
7. 566 − 116 =	**8.** 645 − 340 =
9. 465 − 138 =	**10.** 394 − 148 =

THOUSANDS

Here is the warehouse of Frank's Engine Oil Company.

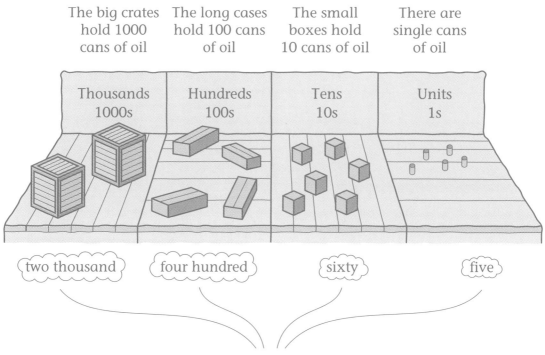

The big crates hold 1000 cans of oil

The long cases hold 100 cans of oil

The small boxes hold 10 cans of oil

There are single cans of oil

| Thousands 1000s | Hundreds 100s | Tens 10s | Units 1s |

two thousand   four hundred   sixty   five

There are **2465** cans of oil in total.

Exercise 3

Write down how many cans of oil are in the warehouse each day.

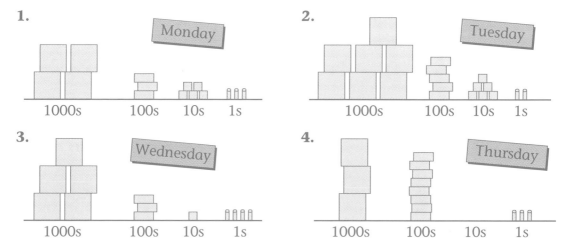

1. Monday — 1000s 100s 10s 1s

2. Tuesday — 1000s 100s 10s 1s

3. Wednesday — 1000s 100s 10s 1s

4. Thursday — 1000s 100s 10s 1s

Exercise 4

Draw these numbers of oil cans, like the drawings in Exercise 3.
1. 3152   **2.** 1526   **3.** 6142   **4.** 3502

Exercise 5

Write out these orders in figures.

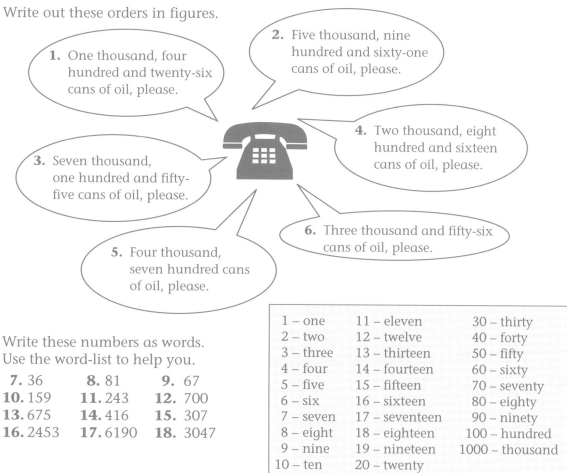

1. One thousand, four hundred and twenty-six cans of oil, please.

2. Five thousand, nine hundred and sixty-one cans of oil, please.

3. Seven thousand, one hundred and fifty-five cans of oil, please.

4. Two thousand, eight hundred and sixteen cans of oil, please.

5. Four thousand, seven hundred cans of oil, please.

6. Three thousand and fifty-six cans of oil, please.

Write these numbers as words.
Use the word-list to help you.

7. 36   **8.** 81   **9.** 67
10. 159   **11.** 243   **12.** 700
13. 675   **14.** 416   **15.** 307
16. 2453   **17.** 6190   **18.** 3047

1 – one	11 – eleven	30 – thirty
2 – two	12 – twelve	40 – forty
3 – three	13 – thirteen	50 – fifty
4 – four	14 – fourteen	60 – sixty
5 – five	15 – fifteen	70 – seventy
6 – six	16 – sixteen	80 – eighty
7 – seven	17 – seventeen	90 – ninety
8 – eight	18 – eighteen	100 – hundred
9 – nine	19 – nineteen	1000 – thousand
10 – ten	20 – twenty	

Exercise 6

There are **4537** cans of oil in the warehouse.

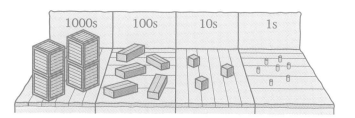

1. If **3341** cans were **added**, how many cans would there be in total?

2. If **3415** cans were **taken away**, how many cans would be left?

3. If **4032** were **added**, how many cans would there be in total?

4. If **2124** cans were **taken away**, how many cans would be left?

5. If **1420** were **added**, how many cans would there be in total?

HARDER ADDITION (+)

Work these out in your head.
Spend 15 minutes on each card; see how many you can complete.

Addition workcard 5	Addition workcard 6	Addition workcard 7
1. 140 + 37 + 121 =	**1.** 355 + 1410 =	**1.** 4288 + 2243 =
2. 61 + 105 + 33 =	**2.** 2236 + 522 =	**2.** 2357 + 5257 =
3. 100 + 23 + 9 =	**3.** 547 + 1142 =	**3.** 1884 + 3057 =
4. 28 + 132 + 7 =	**4.** 606 + 1752 =	**4.** 2852 + 1398 =
5. 66 + 118 + 15 =	**5.** 726 + 2423 =	**5.** 2582 + 2639 =
6. 212 + 8 + 37 =	**6.** 1525 + 862 =	**6.** 1958 + 2074 =
7. 250 + 128 + 19 =	**7.** 2918 + 528 =	**7.** 2535 + 3595 =
8. 34 + 106 + 120 =	**8.** 1539 + 623 =	**8.** 6816 + 1886 =
9. 411 + 9 + 154 =	**9.** 856 + 816 =	**9.** 3658 + 2642 =
10. 116 + 118 + 42 =	**10.** 764 + 592 =	**10.** 5882 + 2819 =
11. 306 + 62 + 160 =	**11.** 788 + 450 =	**11.** 1943 + 2057 =
12. 227 + 10 + 181 =	**12.** 692 + 828 =	**12.** 5174 + 1826 =

Exercise 7

1. In a talent contest, the first act gets 61 votes; the second act gets 121 votes and the third act gets 314 votes. What was the total number of votes?

2. On the first day Nazia drove 1225 km, and on the second day 643 km. How many kilometres did she drive in total?

3. 1740 people saw the play on Monday and 1253 on Tuesday. How many people in total saw the play?

4. Three aircraft land. They carry 210 passengers, 64 passengers and 155 passengers. How many passengers were there in total?

5. 604 cars travel South over the bridge, and 1516 travel North. How many cars crossed the bridge?

6. 1351 fans support Carlton F.C. and 8270 fans support Millfield F.C. How many fans are there in the stadium?

7. In three cricket matches, Hicham scores 33, 51 and 130. How many runs does he score in total?

8. Clare swims 830 m on the first day. On the next day she swims 2550 m. How many metres did Clare swim in total?

HARDER SUBTRACTION (−)

Work these out in your head.
Spend 15 minutes on each card; see how many you can complete.

Subtraction workcard 5	Subtraction workcard 6	Subtraction workcard 7
1. 250 − 116 =	**1.** 3525 − 2415 =	**1.** 6523 −　166 =
2. 725 − 505 =	**2.** 6505 − 1400 =	**2.** 3582 −　576 =
3. 960 − 239 =	**3.** 3660 − 2369 =	**3.** 4220 −　600 =
4. 607 − 436 =	**4.** 2542 − 1416 =	**4.** 5413 − 2413 =
5. 405 − 115 =	**5.** 6850 − 4536 =	**5.** 3232 − 1232 =
6. 500 − 270 =	**6.** 9633 − 6017 =	**6.** 2583 −　503 =
7. 403 − 153 =	**7.** 8836 − 5163 =	**7.** 6631 − 4714 =
8. 560 − 159 =	**8.** 6915 − 2565 =	**8.** 5280 − 1715 =
9. 304 − 124 =	**9.** 4704 − 2340 =	**9.** 4704 − 2316 =
10. 300 − 160 =	**10.** 6732 − 1156 =	**10.** 5342 − 2565 =
11. 430 − 125 =	**11.** 3940 − 1056 =	**11.** 3320 −　659 =
12. 370 − 264 =	**12.** 6611 − 3235 =	**12.** 2123 −　578 =

Exercise 8

1. There are 23 people on a bus. 17 people get off. How many are left?

2. There are 32 sweets in a box. If 15 are eaten, how many are left?

3. There are 41 pupils in a room. If 9 pupils leave, how many are left?

4. Victoria has 65p. She spends 18p. How much has she got left?

5. Mary has 74 buttons in a tin. She takes out 9. How many buttons are left in the tin?

6. A lorry carries 100 boxes. If 43 are unloaded, how many are left?

7. A match box holds 145 matches. 54 of the matches are used. How many matches are left?

8. A shop keeper orders 235 bags of crisps. He sells 182 bags. How many bags of crisps are left?

9. A ferry carries 3638 passengers. 831 passengers get off at the first stop. How many passengers are left on the ferry?

10. Liam has 1307 comics. He gives away 38 comics. How many comics has he got left?

MULTIPLICATION (×)

Here are four containers.
In each container there are 3 tennis balls.
To find the total number of tennis balls you could:

    a   count each ball to give a total of   12
    b   or add 4 lots of 3 = 3 + 3 + 3 + 3 = 12
    c   or remember that 3 × 4 = 12

Exercise 9

Show each of these drawings as a sum, and work out the answer.

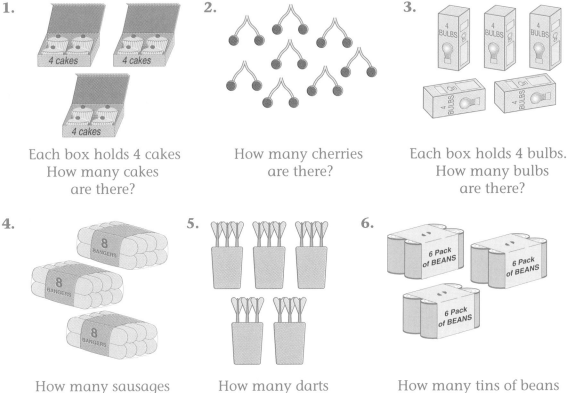

1.

Each box holds 4 cakes
How many cakes
are there?

2.

How many cherries
are there?

3.

Each box holds 4 bulbs.
How many bulbs
are there?

4.

How many sausages
are there?

5.

How many darts
are there?

6.

How many tins of beans
are there?

Exercise 10

Copy and complete these statements. Question **1** is done for you.

  1. 4 lots of 2 = 8   **2.** 3 lots of 3 =   **3.** 5 lots of 2 =
  4. 4 lots of 3 =   **5.** 4 lots of 4 =   **6.** 6 lots of 2 =
  7. 3 lots of 5 =   **8.** 2 lots of 7 =   **9.** 2 lots of 8 =
10. 2 × 5 =   **11.** 3 × 4 =   **12.** 6 × 3 =
13. 4 × 3 =   **14.** 2 × 6 =   **15.** 7 × 3 =
16. 5 × 5 =   **17.** 6 × 5 =   **18.** 2 × 10 =

Exercise 11

1. What is 3 times 10?
2. What is 5 multiplied by 6?
3. What is 12 times 2?
4. What do 4 lots of 6 make?
5. What do 7 lots of 4 make?
6. What is 9 multiplied by 3?
7. What do 8 groups of 4 make?
8. What is 4 multiplied by 11?
9. What is 10 times 5?
10. What do 7 lots of 5 make?
11. What do 12 groups of 3 make?
12. What is 2 times 16?

Do these in your head.
Spend 10 minutes on each card; see how many you can do in this time.

Multiplication workcard 1

1. $3 \times 4 =$
2. $5 \times 3 =$
3. $4 \times 2 =$
4. $4 \times 5 =$
5. $8 \times 2 =$
6. $3 \times 7 =$
7. $6 \times 3 =$
8. $5 \times 5 =$
9. $3 \times 10 =$
10. $10 \times 5 =$

Multiplication workcard 2

1. $6 \times 6 =$
2. $4 \times 8 =$
3. $4 \times 10 =$
4. $8 \times 5 =$
5. $6 \times 10 =$
6. $2 \times 12 =$
7. $3 \times 13 =$
8. $10 \times 5 =$
9. $21 \times 3 =$
10. $12 \times 3 =$

Multiplication workcard 3

1. $3 \times 22 =$
2. $24 \times 2 =$
3. $2 \times 31 =$
4. $3 \times 23 =$
5. $31 \times 3 =$
6. $20 \times 4 =$
7. $34 \times 2 =$
8. $2 \times 41 =$
9. $13 \times 3 =$
10. $33 \times 3 =$

Multiplication workcard 4

1. $3 \times 17 =$
2. $13 \times 4 =$
3. $15 \times 5 =$
4. $3 \times 24 =$
5. $23 \times 4 =$
6. $2 \times 27 =$
7. $14 \times 5 =$
8. $7 \times 12 =$
9. $26 \times 3 =$
10. $3 \times 27 =$

Multiplication workcard 5

1. $213 \times 2 =$
2. $142 \times 2 =$
3. $232 \times 3 =$
4. $143 \times 2 =$
5. $231 \times 3 =$
6. $125 \times 3 =$
7. $214 \times 4 =$
8. $216 \times 3 =$
9. $127 \times 2 =$
10. $215 \times 4 =$

DIVISION   (÷)

Example 1

Here are   shared into   There will be 4
12 buttons . . .   3 groups . . .   buttons in each group.

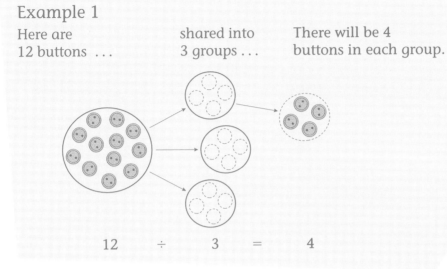

12   ÷   3   =   4

Exercise 12

How many buttons will there be in each group?

1. 15 buttons shared by 3.   **2.** 16 buttons shared by 4.   **3.** 24 buttons shared by 6.

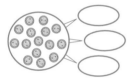  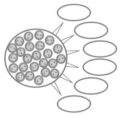

Exercise 13

Copy and complete these division sums.

1. Share 10 sweets into 2 groups.

   10 ÷ 2 = ☐

2. Share 12 cakes into 4 groups.

   12 ÷ 4 = ☐

3. Share 16 pence into 2 groups.

   16 ÷ 2 = ☐

4. Share 15 apples into 3 groups.

   15 ÷ 3 = ☐

5. Share 24 pencils into 4 groups.

   24 ÷ 4 = ☐

6. Share 21 pies into 3 groups.

21 ÷ 3 = ☐

7. If 3 people share 18 books, how many do they each get?
8. If 5 people share 15 cakes, how many do they each get?
9. If 4 children share 16 comics, how many do they each get?
10. If 6 children share 18 marbles, how many do they each get?
11. If 3 children share 24 sweets, how many do they each get?
12. 4 children share £20. How much do they each get?

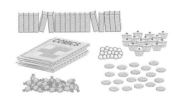

Exercise 14

1. This gate is made from 5 pieces of wood.
How many gates can be made from:
   a 15 pieces of wood
   b 30 pieces of wood
   c 45 pieces of wood
   d 75 pieces of wood?

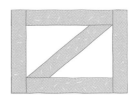

2 Each box holds 10 biscuits.
How many boxes can be filled with:
   a 30 biscuits
   b 70 biscuits
   c 50 biscuits
   d 100 biscuits?

Exercise 15

Work these out in your head. How many can you do in 10 minutes?

Division workcard 1

1. $6 \div 2 =$	**2.** $8 \div 4 =$	**3.** $6 \div 3 =$	**4.** $10 \div 5 =$	**5.** $8 \div 2 =$
6. $12 \div 2 =$	**7.** $10 \div 2 =$	**8.** $12 \div 4 =$	**9.** $20 \div 5 =$	**10.** $12 \div 3 =$

Division workcard 2

1. $14 \div 2 =$	**2.** $15 \div 3 =$	**3.** $16 \div 4 =$	**4.** $20 \div 4 =$	**5.** $14 \div 7 =$
6. $18 \div 9 =$	**7.** $20 \div 2 =$	**8.** $18 \div 2 =$	**9.** $16 \div 2 =$	**10.** $15 \div 5 =$

Division workcard 3

1. $30 \div 3 =$	**2.** $20 \div 4 =$	**3.** $20 \div 10 =$	**4.** $40 \div 5 =$	**5.** $30 \div 10 =$
6. $60 \div 10 =$	**7.** $50 \div 2 =$	**8.** $30 \div 6 =$	**9.** $40 \div 2 =$	**10.** $50 \div 5 =$

Division workcard 4

1. $26 \div 2 =$	**2.** $28 \div 4 =$	**3.** $36 \div 6 =$	**4.** $33 \div 3 =$	**5.** $40 \div 8 =$
6. $35 \div 7 =$	**7.** $48 \div 4 =$	**8.** $49 \div 7 =$	**9.** $64 \div 8 =$	**10.** $100 \div 10 =$

7 TRIANGLES

This unit will help you to:
→ **identify and name types of triangle**
→ **construct triangles**
→ **calculate angles in a triangle.**

IDENTIFYING TRIANGLES

Remember a triangle is a shape with 3 straight sides.

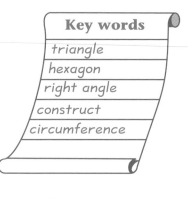

Exercise 1

Look at the shapes below, and decide which of them are triangles.

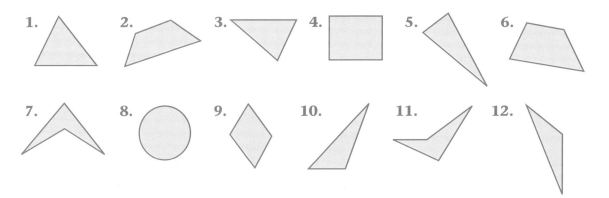

Exercise 2

Look carefully at the shapes below and say how many triangles you can see in each drawing.

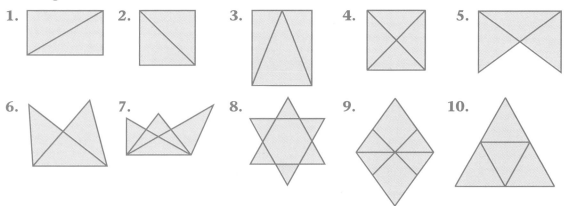

ESTIMATING ANGLES

Example 1

This is a right angle.

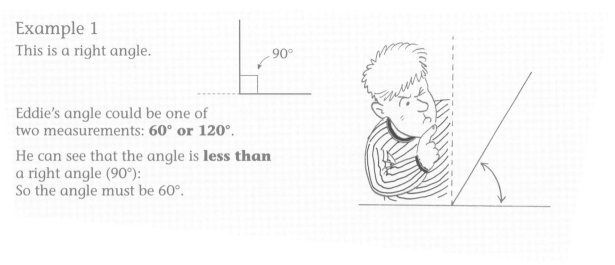

90°

Eddie's angle could be one of
two measurements: **60° or 120°**.

He can see that the angle is **less than**
a right angle (90°):
So the angle must be 60°.

Exercise 3

Using what you know about the right angle, decide which measurement best fits
each angle.

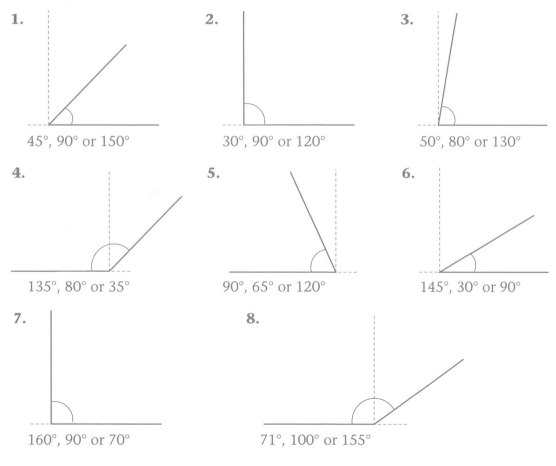

1.

45°, 90° or 150°

2.

30°, 90° or 120°

3.

50°, 80° or 130°

4.

135°, 80° or 35°

5.

90°, 65° or 120°

6.

145°, 30° or 90°

7.

160°, 90° or 70°

8.

71°, 100° or 155°

FAMILIES OF TRIANGLES

This is the family of triangles:

Scalene triangle
The length of each side is different.
The size of each angle is also different.

Isosceles triangle
Two of the sides are the same length.
Two angles are equal in size.

Equilateral triangle
All three sides are the same length.
All three angles are also equal.

Right angle triangle
Has one right angle (90°).
The box in the corner shows the right angle ⟶

Exercise 4

Write down which family each triangle belongs to.
Use a ruler to check your answers.

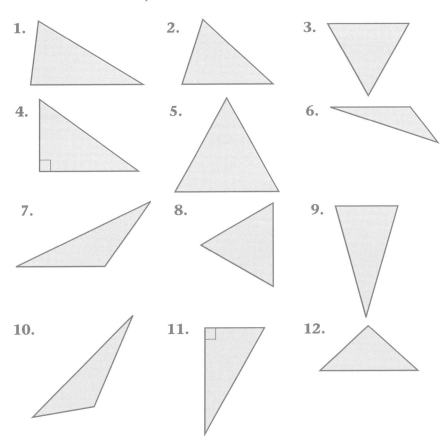

NUMERACY TARGET NUMBERS 180

Exercise 5

This exercise will help with some calculations in the next four exercises.

What number must be added to the number in the shaded bubble so that the total is 180?

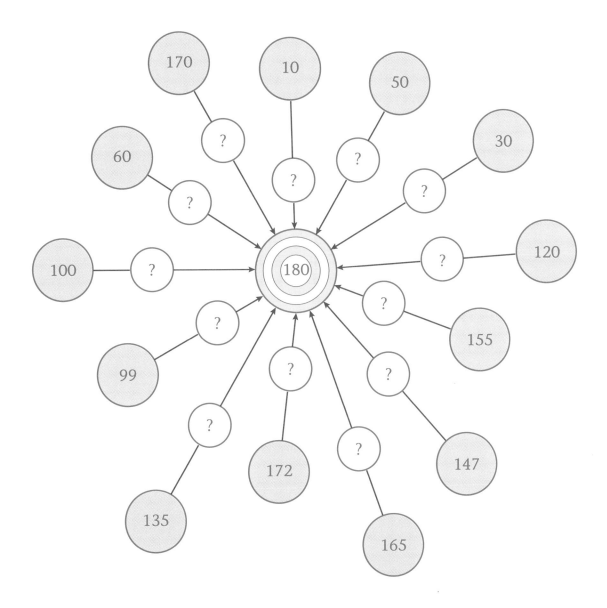

Exercise 6

Use a protractor to measure the angles of these two triangles.
Copy and complete the sentences below.

1. Angle a = ____°

2. Angle b = ____°

3. Angle c = ____°

4. The three angles of the triangle add up to ____°

5. Angle x = ____°

6. Angle y = ____°

7. Angle z = ____°

8. The three angles of the triangle add up to ____°

If you have measured the angles carefully and added accurately, you should notice:
the angles of a triangle add up to 180°.

Exercise 7

Here is a page from Martin's Maths book. He has drawn some triangles and measured their angles, but he has not measured carefully. Which of his answers are wrong?

Triangles   9 May

1. angle a = 65°
   angle b = 55°
   angle c = 60°

2. angle a = 35°
   angle b = 65°
   angle c = 85°

3. angle a = 90°
   angle b = 10°
   angle c = 20°

Triangles   9 May

4. angle a = 100°
   angle b = 70°
   angle c = 20°

5. angle a = 90°
   angle b = 10°
   angle c = 52°

6. angle a = 73°
   angle b = 24°
   angle c = 83°

7. angle a = 113°
   angle b = 14°
   angle c = 53°

9. angle a = 15°
   angle b = 117°
   angle c = 68°

10. angle a = 27°
    angle b = 92°
    angle c = 51°

11. angle a = 49°
    angle b = 61°
    angle c = 70°

FINDING MISSING ANGLES

The angles of a triangle add up to 180°.

Example 2

If you know two of the angles, you can find
the third angle.

angle a + 60° + 70° = 180°

So, angle a = 50°

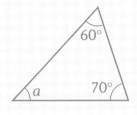

Exercise 8

Work out the size of the angles marked with a letter.
Do not measure the angles.

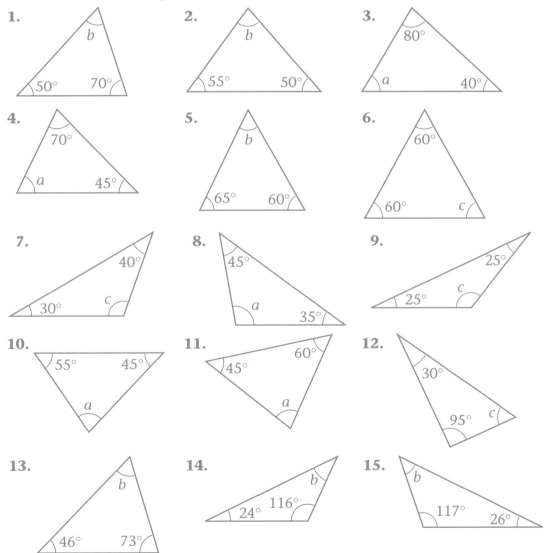

ANGLES ON A LINE

The angles in a triangle
and
angles on a straight line

$$= \boxed{180°}$$

$$a + b + c = 180°$$

$$x + y = 180°$$

ACTIVITY

Cut a triangle out of card, and mark the three angles with stars.

Cut the three angles from the triangle.

Bring the three angles together on a straight line. The angles will add up to a straight angle or 180°.

Exercise 9

Find the angles marked with letters in each question.

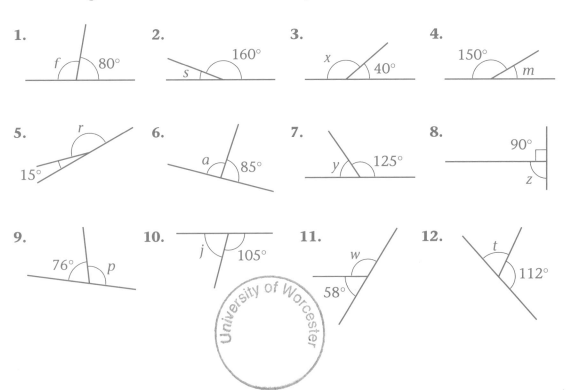

1. f $80°$

2. $160°$ s

3. x $40°$

4. $150°$ m

5. r $15°$

6. a $85°$

7. y $125°$

8. $90°$ z

9. $76°$ p

10. j $105°$

11. w $58°$

12. t $112°$

Example 3

To find both of the unknown angles you must
use two facts: a straight angle = 180°
               angles in a triangle = 180°

angle a = 180° − 110° = 70°
so angle b = 180° − 60° − 70° = 50°

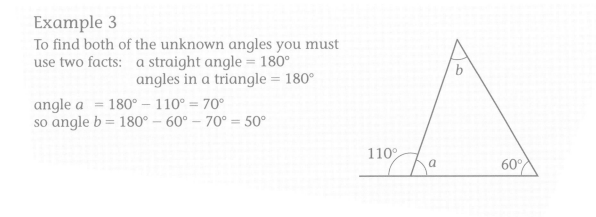

Exercise 10

Find the angles marked with letters.

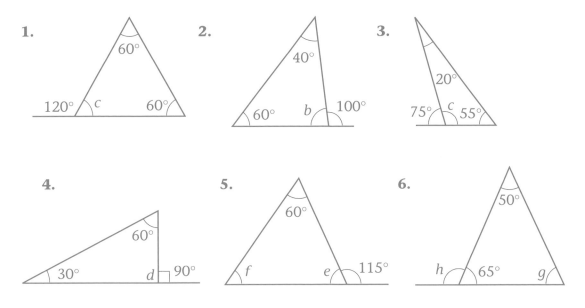

1. 60° 120° c 60°

2. 40° 60° b 100°

3. 20° 75° c 55°

4. 60° 30° d 90°

5. 60° f e 115°

6. 50° h 65° g

Exercise 11

Find the three lettered angles in each question.

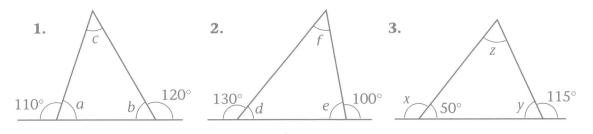

1. c 110° a b 120°

2. f 130° d e 100°

3. z x 50° y 115°

CONSTRUCTING TRIANGLES

Example 4

To draw this triangle accurately, you need
to use a pair of compasses and a ruler.
To construct a triangle accurately, follow
these 3 steps:

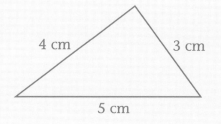

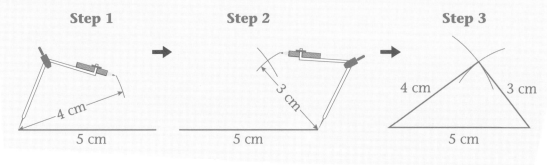

Exercise 12

Use a ruler and compasses to construct accurately the triangles below.
These drawings are not drawn to scale.

1.   **2.**   **3.**

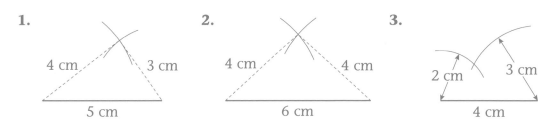

This drawing cannot be finished because
the two arcs will never cross.

For a triangle to be possible, the two shorter
sides must add to more than the largest side.

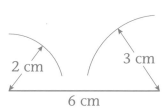

Exercise 13

Say which sets of measurements below would not form triangles if they were
drawn.

1. 2 cm, 4 cm, 5 cm.   **2.** 5 cm, 2 cm, 1 cm.   **3.** 9 cm, 4 cm, 6 cm.

4. 10 cm, 5 cm, 5 cm.   **5.** 15 cm, 7 cm, 6 cm.   **6.** 4 cm, 11 cm, 8 cm.

A**CT**IVITY CONSTRUCTING A REGULAR HEXAGON

A hexagon is a six-sided shape.
A **regular** hexagon is a six-sided shape, with all its sides and angles equal.

1. Follow these steps to draw a regular hexagon:

Step 1.

Set your compasses to 5 cm and draw a circle.

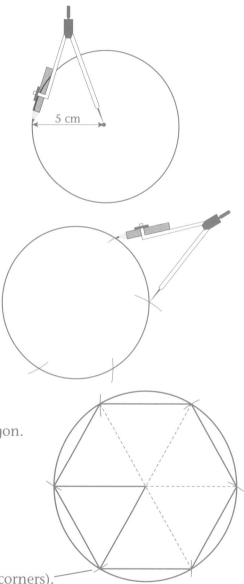

Step 2.

DO NOT ADJUST THE COMPASSES
Use this measurement to make 5 cm marks
around the circumference of the circle.

Step 3.

Now join up the points to complete the hexagon.

Step 4.

Join the centre of the hexagon to its vertices (corners).

2. How many triangles are there in a hexagon?
3. Do you notice anything about the angles?

8 USING DECIMALS

This unit will help you to:
→ **understand and write simple decimal numbers**
→ **understand $\frac{1}{10}$ s and $\frac{1}{100}$ s.**

DECIMAL MEASUREMENTS

The students here are finding out about plants, animals, feathers and other objects.

They measure the items in their collection.

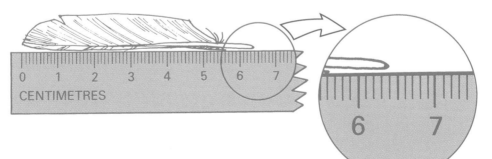

Each centimetre is divided into 10 equal parts.
So each part is one-tenth($\frac{1}{10}$) of a centimetre.

This close-up shows the tenths of a centimetre and the end of the feather.

The feather is 6 cm and 4 tenths of a centimetre.

Exercise 1

This is a table of measurements made by the students.

	Item	cm	tenths of cm
1	Worm	5	9
2	Oak leaf		
3	Beetle		
4	Feather		
5	Earwig		
6	Butterfly		
7	Bluebell Stem		
8	Tadpole		
9	Holly Leaf		
10	Ear of wheat		

Copy the table and fill in the measurements for each close-up.

1. Worm   **2.** Oak leaf   **3.** Beetle   **4.** Feather

5. Earwig   **6.** Butterfly   **7.** Bluebell stem

8. Tadpole   **9.** Holly leaf   **10.** Ear of wheat

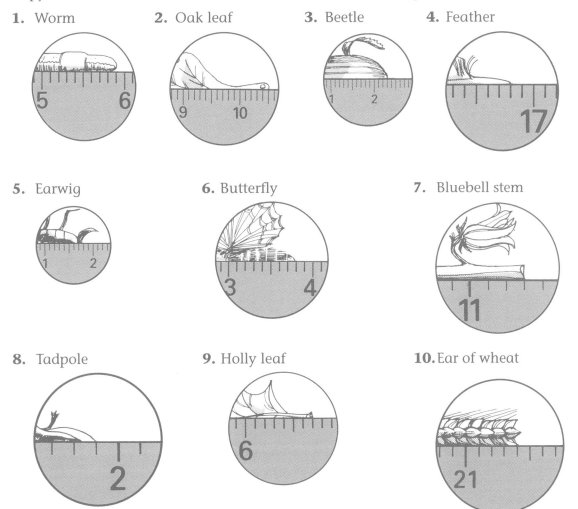

USING THE DECIMAL POINT

Example 1
The feather is 6 cm and 4 tenths of a cm long.

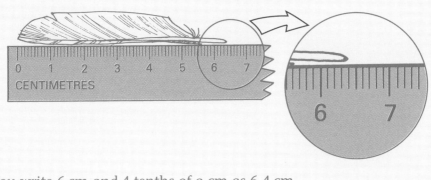

You write 6 cm and 4 tenths of a cm as 6.4 cm.

Exercise 2
Re-draw the table in Exercise 1. This time use the decimal point in the table, Like this:

	Item	Length in cm
1	Worm	5.9 cm
2	Oak leaf	10.5 cm

Exercise 3
Copy and complete the table.

1.	6 cm and 4 tenths	6.4 cm
2.	2 cm and 1 tenth	
3.	5 cm and 0 tenths	5.0 cm
4.	4 cm and 7 tenths	
5.	3 cm and 9 tenths	
6.	8 cm and 8 tenths	
7.	11 cm and 3 tenths	
8.	13 cm and 2 tenths	13.2 cm
9.	7 cm and 0 tenths	
10.	15 cm and 0 tenths	
11.	11 cm and 9 tenths	
12.	54 cm and 3 tenths	
13.	16 cm and 0 tenths	
14.	43 cm and 5 tenths	
15.	16 cm and 6 tenths	
16.	27 cm and 4 tenths	
17.	15 cm and 2 tenths	
18.	70 cm and 0 tenths	
19.	61 cm and 8 tenths	
20.	39 cm and 2 tenths	

Exercise 4

Measure these objects to the nearest tenth of a centimetre.
Make a table like that in Exercise 2.

1. Earthworm

2. Stickleback fish

3. Ear of wheat

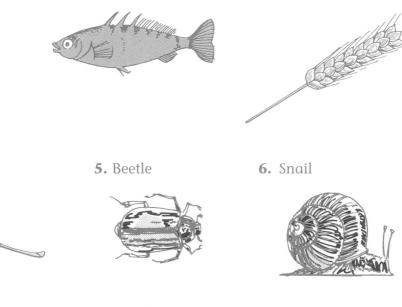

4. Oak leaf

5. Beetle

6. Snail

7. Holly leaf

8. Caterpillar

9. Newt

Exercise 5

Answer these questions about the objects above.

1. Which drawing is exactly 3.0 cm long?
2. Which drawing is 5.4 cm long?
3. Which drawing is 4.4 cm long?
4. Which drawing is 3.2 cm long?
5. Which is longer, the holly leaf or the ear of wheat?
6. Which drawing is exactly 5 cm long?
7. Which is longer, the beetle or the caterpillar?
8. Which is the longest drawing?
9. Which is the shortest drawing?
10. Which drawings are longer than 5 cm?

DECIMALS LESS THAN ONE

The students find some bugs.

The length of this bug is less than a centimetre.

It is 0 cm and 6 tenths of a centimetre long.

This is written as 0.6 cm. You say 'nought-point-six centimetres'.

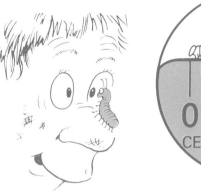

Exercise 6

Copy and complete the table giving the length of the bugs.

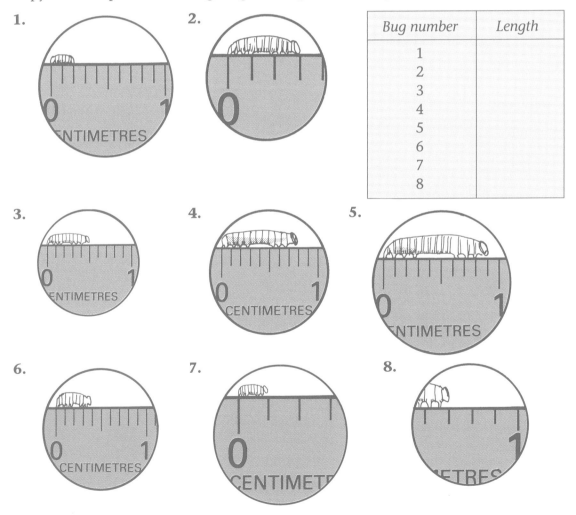

1.

2.

Bug number	Length
1	
2	
3	
4	
5	
6	
7	
8	

3.

4.

5.

6.

7.

8.

TWO DECIMAL PLACES

The pike is more than 0.4 m and less than 0.5 m.

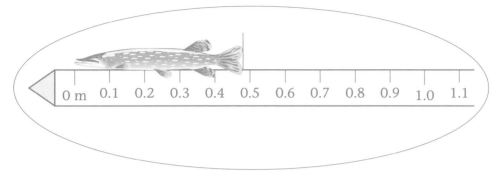

Using a bigger scale, you can measure more accurately.
You can see that the pike is 0.48 m long.

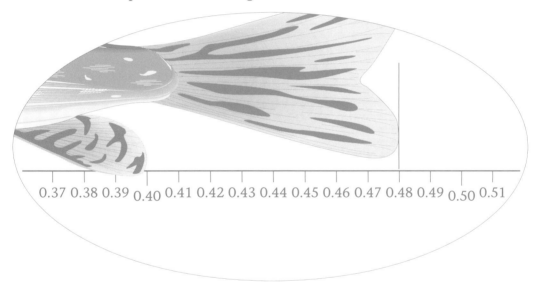

0.48 m has **2 decimal places**, because there are two numbers after the decimal point.

Exercise 7

Use these metre scales to measure to 2 decimal places.

1.

0m 0.01 0.02 0.03 0.04 0.05 0.06 0.07 0.08 0.09 0.1 0.11

2.

1.09 1.10 1.11 1.12 1.13 1.14 1.15 1.16 1.17 1.18 1.19 1.20 1.21 1.22 1.23 1.24 1.25

3.

2.23 2.24 2.25 2.26 2.27 2.28 2.29 2.30 2.31 2.32 2.33 2.34 2.35 2.36 2.37 2.38

Exercise 8

Complete these questions using 2 decimal places.

1. At what position on the decimal scale is the arrow?

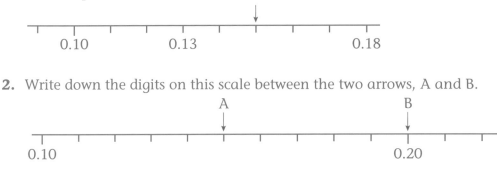

0.10   0.13   0.18

2. Write down the digits on this scale between the two arrows, A and B.

A   B

0.10   0.20

3. Write down a decimal number that is: **a** more than 2.54, **b** less than 2.54.

4. If Jane has £5.20 and Mark has £5.18, who has the most money?

5. Estimate the length of the dotted line using 2 decimal places.

0.10   0.20

6. Which two sticks would you join together to make a total length of 2.54 m.

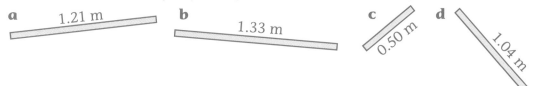

a   1.21 m   **b**   1.33 m   **c** 0.50 m   **d** 1.04 m

7. The width of these cars is written down in 2 decimal places.
The tunnel is 4 m wide.

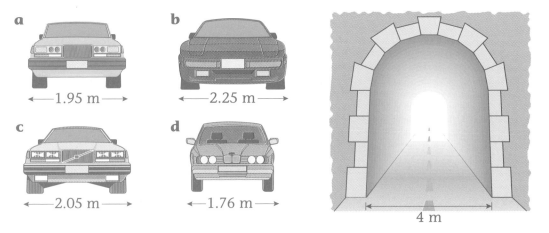

a ←1.95 m→   **b** ←2.25 m→

c ←2.05 m→   **d** ←1.76 m→

4 m

Which cars will fit side-by-side into the tunnel without scraping each other?

Using drawings

A

This square is one whole unit or 1.0

B

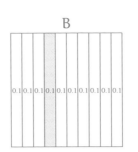

0.1 0.1 0.1 0.1 0.1 0.1 0.1 0.1 0.1 0.1

The whole unit has been divided into ten equal strips. Each strip is a tenth or 0.1.

0.01   C

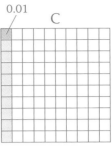

The whole unit has been divided into one hundred equal squares. Each square is a hundredth or 0.01.

Exercise 9

1. Look at diagrams A and B. Which is larger, 0.1 or 1.0?
2. Look at diagram B. How many parts of 0.1 make the whole unit?
3. Look at diagram C. How many 0.01 parts make the whole unit?
4. Look at diagrams B and C. Which is the larger part, 0.1 or 0.01?
5. Look at diagrams B and C. How many 0.01 parts make 0.1?

Exercise 10

Use the diagrams A, B and C above to write down the numbers shown in each drawing. The first one is done for you.

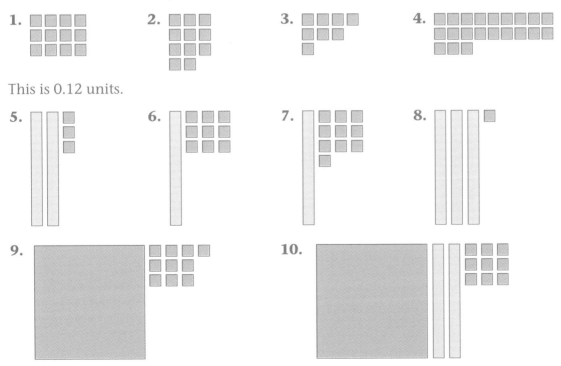

This is 0.12 units.

Here is the square again representing one whole unit.
It has been divided into 100 equal squares.

The part shaded in blue represents eight hundredths.

This is written as: $\frac{8}{100}$ or 0.08

The part shaded in orange is ten hundredths. This is the same as one tenth, so it is written as:

$\frac{10}{100}$ or $\frac{1}{10}$

0.10 or 0.1

Exercise 11

Copy and complete the table.

	Fraction	Decimal
5 hundredths	$\frac{5}{100}$	0.05
2 hundredths	$\frac{2}{100}$	
* hundredths	$\frac{7}{100}$	
3 hundredths		
19 hundredths		0.19
52 hundredths		
* hundredths		0.75
87 hundredths		
* hundredths	$\frac{94}{100}$	
1 whole and 3 hundredths	$1\frac{3}{100}$	1.03
2 wholes and 4 hundredths		
6 wholes and 9 hundredths		
3 wholes and 7 hundredths		
* wholes and * hundredths	$5\frac{21}{100}$	
* wholes and * hundredths		7.50

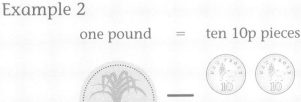

Example 2

one pound   =   ten 10p pieces

10p is one tenth or 0.1 of a pound.

Exercise 12

Copy and complete these sentences. The first one has been done for you.

1. 90p is the same as £0.90
2. 30p is the same as £0.**
3. 60p is the same as £0.**
4. 20p is the same as £0.**
5. 80p is the same as £0.**
6. 50p is the same as £0.**
7. **p is the same as £0.70
8. **p is the same as £0.40
9. **p is the same as £0.10
10. **p is the same as £0.30

Example 3

one pound   =   one hundred 1p pieces

1p is one hundredth or 0.01 of a pound.
3p is three hundredths or 0.03 of a pound.
13p is thirteen hundredths or 0.13 of a pound.

Exercise 13

Copy and complete these sentences. The first two have been done for you.

1. 7p is the same as £0.07   **2.** 23p is the same as £0.23   **3.** 9p is the same as £0.0*
4. 5p is the same as £0.**   **5.** 8p is the same as £0.**   **6.** 6p is the same as £0.**
7. 16p is the same as £0.**   **8.** 27p is the same as £0.**   **9.** 43p is the same as £0.**
10. 61p is the same as £0.**   **11.** *p is the same as £0.02   **12.** *p is the same as £0.04
13. *p is the same as £0.08   **14.** **p is the same as £0.16   **15.** **p is the same as £0.35

REVIEW 1

A. FRACTIONS

For questions **1–5** write down the shaded fraction.

1.   2.   3.   4.   5.

For questions **6–10** match the fraction to the correct drawings.

    a $\frac{2}{3}$ **b** $\frac{3}{4}$ **c** $\frac{2}{5}$ **d** $\frac{4}{5}$ **e** $\frac{3}{10}$

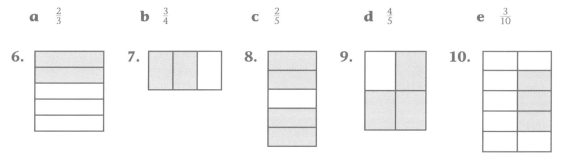

6.   7.   8.   9.   10.

For questions **11** and **12** answer these four questions.

    a   How many parts are there?
    b   What fraction is each part?
    c   What fraction is shaded?
    d   What fraction is unshaded?

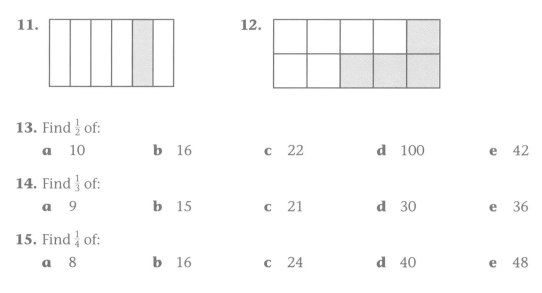

11.   12.

13. Find $\frac{1}{2}$ of:

    a 10   **b** 16   **c** 22   **d** 100   **e** 42

14. Find $\frac{1}{3}$ of:

    a 9   **b** 15   **c** 21   **d** 30   **e** 36

15. Find $\frac{1}{4}$ of:

    a 8   **b** 16   **c** 24   **d** 40   **e** 48

B. Angles

Find the missing angle in each triangle.

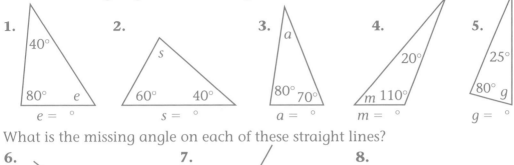

1. 40° 80° e
e = ___°

2. s 60° 40°
s = ___°

3. a 80° 70°
a = ___°

4. 20° m 110°
m = ___°

5. 25° 80° g
g = ___°

What is the missing angle on each of these straight lines?

6. r 140°

7. m 60°

8. 32° t

C. Decimal Measurement

What are the lengths of these objects?

1. This toy soldier is 4.8 cm long.

4   5

2. This stamp is ___ cm long.

20p
2   3

3. This match is ___ cm long.

4   5

4. This spark plug is ___ cm long.

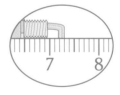

7   8

5. This clip is ___ cm long.

1   2

Measure these lines accurately.

6. |———————————|

7. |————————————————|

8. |——————|

9. |——————————————|

10. |————|

D. TIME

How long is there between the times shown on these clocks?

1. Start   Finish

2. Start   Finish

3. Start   Finish

Copy and complete these sentences, a.m. or p.m.

4. 06.00 is the same as 6 ____   **5.** 13.00 is the same as 1 ____

6. 18.15 is the same as 6.15 ____   **7.** 09.00 is the same as 9 ____

8. 11.00 is the same as 11 ____   **9.** 22.30 is the same as 10.30 ____

10. Write the months of the year in the correct order beginning with January.

January	June	September	November
August	May	July	April
December	February	March	October

11. Answer the questions about the timeline.

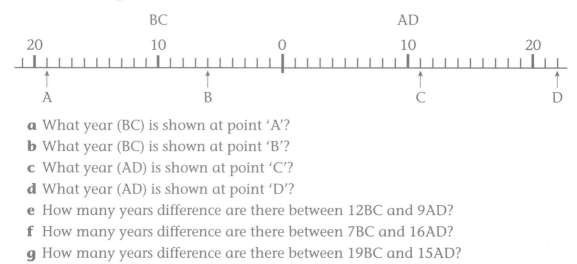

    a What year (BC) is shown at point 'A'?

    b What year (BC) is shown at point 'B'?

    c What year (AD) is shown at point 'C'?

    d What year (AD) is shown at point 'D'?

    e How many years difference are there between 12BC and 9AD?

    f How many years difference are there between 7BC and 16AD?

    g How many years difference are there between 19BC and 15AD?

E. MULTIPLYING AND DIVIDING BY 10

1. Multiply each of these numbers by 10.
(Do them as quickly as you can in your head.)

a	4	**b**	8	**c**	9	**d**	13	**e**	18
f	21	**g**	26	**h**	47	**i**	100	**j**	231

2. Problems involving × 10s

    a Cara has 7 photo albums. Each album can hold 10 photographs. How many photographs can she put into the albums?

    b Ahmed gets £10 a week for working in the market. How much will Ahmed earn during 14 weeks?

    c There are 24 students in Mr Allan's class. For homework they each do 10 sums. How many sums does Mr Allan have to mark?

3. Divide each of these numbers by 10.
(Do them as quickly as you can in your head.)

a	30	**b**	50	**c**	70	**d**	90	**e**	100
f	120	**g**	160	**h**	230	**i**	290	**j**	450

4. Problems involving ÷ 10s

    a Sean uses 10 sheets of newspaper to make a papier-mâché mask. How many masks can he make with 70 sheets of paper?

    b To make each cake Rosie uses 10 grams of sugar. How many cakes can she make using 150 grams of sugar?

    c Melinda makes one phone call for 10p. How many phone calls can she make with £2.30?

F. CONGRUENCE

1. Which of these shapes are congruent to each other? There are more than two.

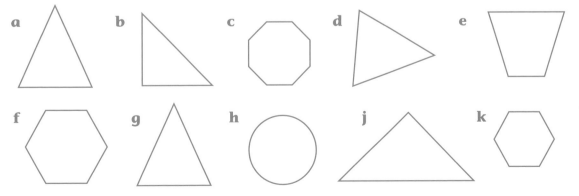

2. Which of the shapes will tessellate?

⑨ POSITION

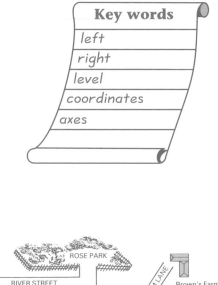

Key words

left
right
level
coordinates
axes

This unit will help you to:
→ **give and find location**
→ **understand and use coordinates.**

DIRECTIONS

Exercise 1

Look at the map.
Imagine you are standing at '**✗**'.

1. Which road leads to Rose Park?
2. Which road is second on the left?
3. Which road is first on the left?
4. Which road is third on the right?
5. Which road is fourth on the right?
6. Where will you be if you take the second turning on the right and then the first on the left?
7. Where will you be if you take the first turning on the right and then the first on the left?
8. Where will you be if you take the second turning on the left and then the first on the right?

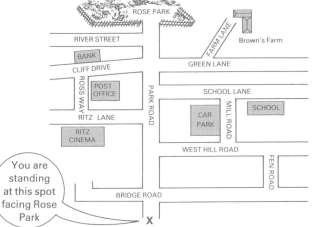

How to give directions:
The way to the Ritz Cinema: Walk up Park Road. Take the second turning on the left. The cinema is on your left.

Exercise 2

Look at the map above. Imagine you are standing at '**✗**'.

1. Give directions to the bank.
2. Give directions to Brown's Farm.
3. Give directions to the school.
4. Give directions to the Post Office.
5. Starting at the Ritz Cinema, give directions to the school.
6. Starting at the school, give directions to Brown's Farm.
7. Starting at the Post Office, give directions to the car park.

Here is the block of flats at Gladstone House.

A window has been broken in one of the flats.

The caretaker says it is the window that is 2 from the left and 3 levels up.

You can describe the position of any window.

Mr Cross is selling his flat. His window is 1 from the left and 2 levels up.

Exercise 3

1. What will you find in the window 2 from the left, 2 levels up?
2. What will you find in the window 5 from the left, 4 levels up?
3. What will you find in the window 1 from the left, 3 levels up?
4. What will you find in the window 3 from the left, 4 levels up?
5. What will you find in the window 5 from the left, 2 levels up?
6. What will you find in the window 1 from the left, 4 levels up?
7. What will you find in the window 3 from the left, 3 levels up?
8. What will you find in the window 4 from the left, 2 levels up?

Now look at the flats at Court View.
Write down these locations.

9. The window with the light.
10. The window with the curtains.
11. The window with the flower.
12. The window with blinds.
13. The window with the boy waving.
14. The broken window.
15. The window of the flat that is for sale.

Exercise 4

The seating plan is for the Economy cabin, on a flight to New York.

Mr Radia has a seat booked. His seat is in column G, row 12. His ticket will have G12 written on it.

Copy out the passenger list. Put each passenger's seat number beside the name.

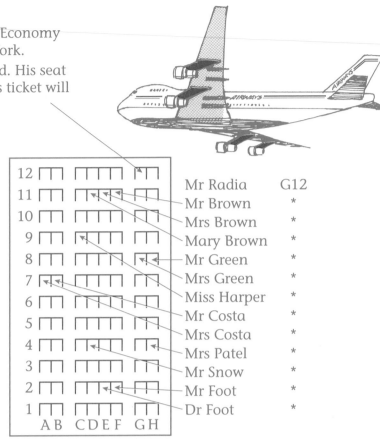

Mr Radia	G12
Mr Brown	*
Mrs Brown	*
Mary Brown	*
Mr Green	*
Mrs Green	*
Miss Harper	*
Mr Costa	*
Mrs Costa	*
Mrs Patel	*
Mr Snow	*
Mr Foot	*
Dr Foot	*

Exercise 5

These passengers arrive late.
Give the name of the passenger next to them on the flight to New York.

1. Mr Smart is given seat E4.
2. Miss Jay is given seat G4.
3. Mr Cross is given seat H12.
4. Mrs Bath is given seat D2.
5. Ms Cole is given seat D9.
6. Dr Lee is given seat C11.

Exercise 6

Here is the seating plan for the First Class cabin on the New York flight. Copy it out and show where each passenger is sitting using arrows.

Mr Khan	F7
Mrs Khan	E7
Ms Franks	B6
Mr Grey	D6
Mr Gill	C5
Mrs Gill	D5
Dr Cross	F4
Miss Fox	A3
Mr Cave	C1
Mrs Cave	C2

COORDINATES

A coordinate is a pair of numbers that fixes a position on a grid. In the diagram, the letter *e* has coordinates (2, 6).

2 across   6 up

Remember: The first number is 'across'.
            The second number is 'up'.

Exercise 7

Can you spell out the tongue-twister shown by the coordinates below?
The first coordinate is (6,1) which is '*r*'.
(6,1), (7,6), (1,3)
(5,3), (2,6), (3,4), (7,4), (4,2), (7,6), (2,7)
(6,5), (2,6), (1,2), (5,3), (8,1), (3,1)
(1,2), (7,6), (7,0), (1,5), (4,2), (2,6), (6,1)

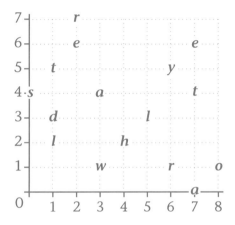

Exercise 8

Look carefully at this map. Then answer the questions.
Write down what you will find at:

1. the coordinates (8,6)
2. the coordinates (1,9)
3. the coordinates (9,8)
4. the coordinates (4,5)
5. the coordinates (2,4).

Give the coordinates for:

6. the roundabout
7. the lighthouse
8. the dock
9. the station
10. the boat
11. the level crossing
12. Sty Farm
13. the castle
14. Pond Farm
15. the bridge

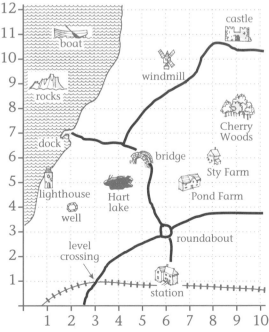

GRIDS

Example 1

These axes are numbered 1–5.
The vertical (↕) axis is the *y*-axis.
The horizontal (↔) axis is the *x*-axis.
The corners of the triangle are A, B and C.

    A is 1 across and 2 up.
    B is 3 across and 4 up.
    C is 4 across and 1 up.

To save time, we write the positions like this:

    A(1,2) B(3,4) C(4,1)

These numbers are called coordinates.
    The first number is 'across'.
    The second number is 'up'.

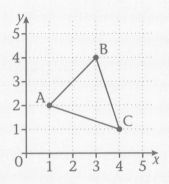

Exercise 9

1 **a** What is the position of R? (__, __)
    b What is the position of A? (__, __)
    c What is the position of Y? (__, __)

2 **a** What are the coordinates of P?
    b What are the coordinates of A?
    c What are the coordinates of T?

3. Write the coordinates of each letter.
    M (__, __) A (__, __) T (__, __)
    H (__, __) S (__, __) W (__, __)
    O (__, __) R (__, __) K (__, __)

4. What letters will you find at:
    a (10,6)   **b** (1,6)
    c (9,1)   **d** (9,3)?

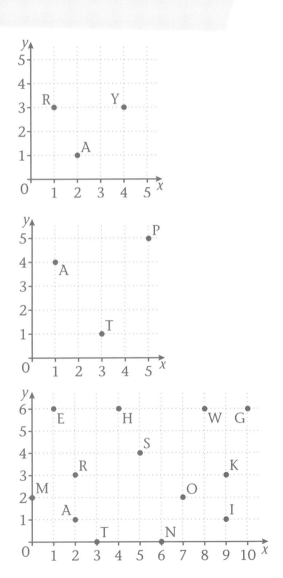

Exercise 10

1. **a** Give four coordinates which are on the green line.
   b Give four coordinates which are to the left of the line.
   c. Give four coordinates which are to the right of the line.

2. **a** What are the coordinates of the corners A, B, C and D?
   b Give five coordinates which are outside the rectangle.
   c Give four coordinates which are inside the rectangle.

3. **a** Give four coordinates which are on the circle.
   b Give four coordinates which are outside the circle.
   c Give three coordinates which are inside the circle.
   d What are the coordinates of the centre of the circle?

4. **a** Give four coordinates which are above the green line.
   b Give four coordinates which are below the green line.
   c Give four coordinates which are on the green line.
   d Write down four more coordinates which would be on the green line if it was drawn longer.

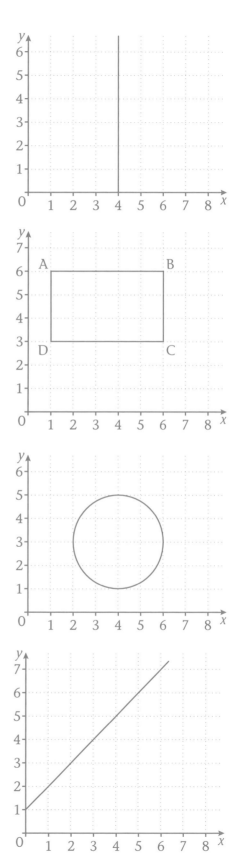

Exercise 11

1. **a** Give coordinates for points A, B, C and D.
   b Give the next four coordinates to continue the pattern on these axes.

2. Give the next four coordinates to continue the pattern on these axes.

3. **a** Give coordinates for points A, B, C, D and E.
   b. Give the next four coordinates to continue the pattern on these axes.

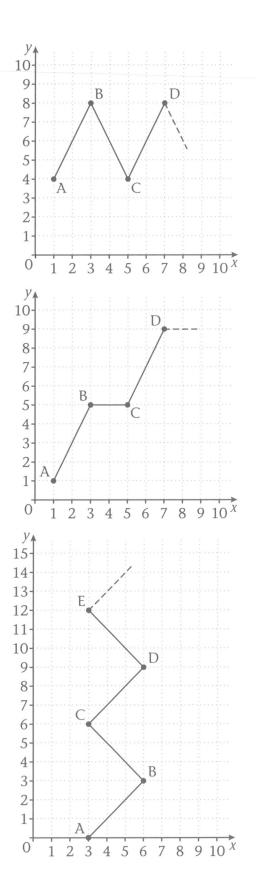

This picture has been drawn using
the following coordinates.
(14,6), (11,2), (10,1), (5,1), (4,2),
(2,3), (2,6), (4,6), (5,7), (7,8), (7,9),
(8,9), (8,8), (10,7), (11,6), (11,5),
(13,6), (14,6).
(4,3), (4,5), (3,5), (3,3), (4,3)

Remember: the first number is
'across', the second
number is 'up'.

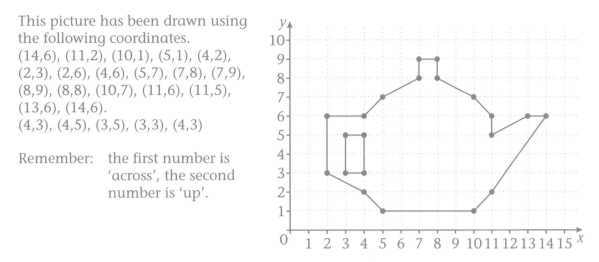

Exercise 12

Draw out the following grids on squared paper. Plot the coordinates. Then draw a
picture by joining up the points in the order you plotted them.

1. (10,3), (9,1), (3,1), (1,3), (10,3),
(6,11), (6,3), (5,4), (1,4), (6,10).

2. (12,13), (9,12), (8,13), (7,17), (7,19),
(6,20), (5,20), (4,19), (1,17), (5,18), (6,17),
(7,11), (7,9), (10,7), (10,2), (7,1), (11,1),
(10,2), (12,8), (14,9), (15,11), (15,16),
(14,12), (12,13).

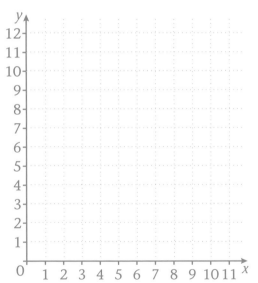

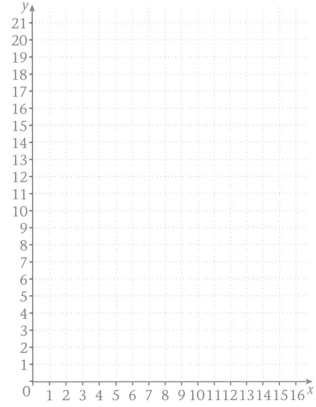

⑩ DISTANCE

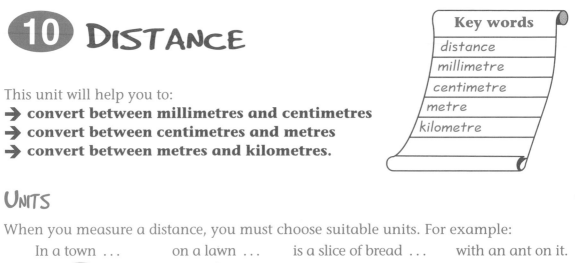

Key words

distance

millimetre

centimetre

metre

kilometre

This unit will help you to:
→ **convert between millimetres and centimetres**
→ **convert between centimetres and metres**
→ **convert between metres and kilometres.**

UNITS

When you measure a distance, you must choose suitable units. For example:

In a town ...   on a lawn ...   is a slice of bread ...   with an ant on it.

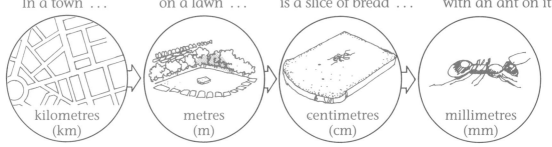

kilometres (km)   metres (m)   centimetres (cm)   millimetres (mm)

The choice of unit depends on the size or distance to be measured.
For example:

In 1978 Hans Mulkin crawled 2560 km to see the President in Washington. Sadly, the President was too busy.

The world's highest waterfall, The Angel Falls in Venezuela is 972 m in height.

The world's shortest male dwarf, Calvin Philips, was only 67 cm tall.

The smallest adult fish the Dwarf Goby is about 9 mm long

Exercise 1

Decide which units you would use to measure these distances.
Write: millimetres, centimetres, metres or kilometres.
  1. The length of your foot.   **2.** The height of your house.
  3. The length of an eye lash.   **4.** The distance around the world.
  5. The distance around your head. **6.** The width of a pencil.
  7. The distance from your school to the South Pole.
  8. The distance from your home to school.
  9. The distance around your wrist.   **10.** Your height.

Each centimetre is divided into ten equal parts.

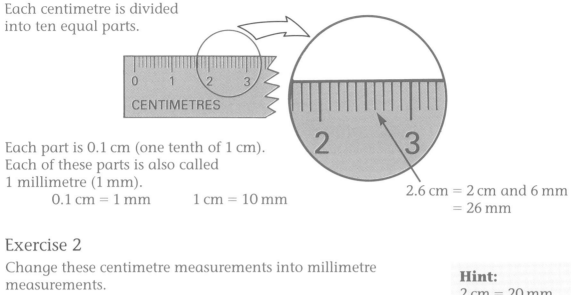

Each part is 0.1 cm (one tenth of 1 cm).
Each of these parts is also called
1 millimetre (1 mm).

$$0.1 \text{ cm} = 1 \text{ mm} \qquad 1 \text{ cm} = 10 \text{ mm}$$

2.6 cm = 2 cm and 6 mm
= 26 mm

Exercise 2

Change these centimetre measurements into millimetre measurements.

1. 1 cm =   **2.** 2 cm =   **3.** 4 cm =   **4.** 5 cm =
5. 7 cm =   **6.** 2.5 cm =   **7.** 3.5 cm =   **8.** 6.5 cm =
9. 4.2 cm =   **10.** 3.4 cm =   **11.** 9.7 cm =   **12.** 10 cm =

Hint:
2 cm = 20 mm
2.5 cm = 25 mm

Exercise 3

Change these millimetre measurements into centimetre measurements.

1. 80 mm =   **2.** 90 mm =   **3.** 20 mm =   **4.** 40 mm =
5. 30 mm =   **6.** 60 mm =   **7.** 15 mm =   **8.** 25 mm =
9. 47 mm =   **10.** 92 mm =   **11.** 87 mm =   **12.** 100 mm =

Hint:
80 mm = 8 cm
15 mm = 1.5 cm

Exercise 4

In each of the drawings, guess which of the lettered lines is the longest.
Now check your guesses with a ruler and complete the table.

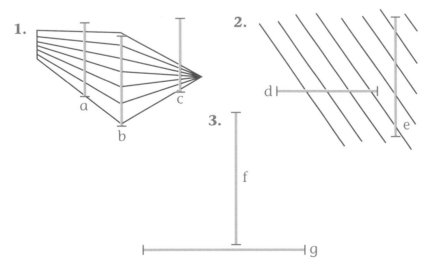

Line	cm
a	
b	
c	
d	
e	
f	
g	

MEASUREMENTS IN METRES

This is a Great White Shark.

These fish grow up to 11 m long.

 A person who is thirteen years old would be just a little longer than the shark's tail.

Exercise 5

Guess the lengths or heights of these animals in metres. You can check them with the world records† shown below.

1. The largest python.   **2.** The longest crocodile.
3. The tallest giraffe.   **4.** The largest Blue Whale.
5. The longest dinosaur.   **6.** The longest lobster caught.

Remember: there are 100 centimetres in 1 metre.
            1 m = 100 cm or 100 cm = 1 m.

Exercise 6

Change these metre measurements to centimetre measurements.

1. 1 m =   **2.** 2 m =   **3.** 4 m =   **4.** 3 m =
5. 6 m =   **6.** 8 m =   **7.** 9 m =   **8.** 4.2 m =
9. 5.5 m =   **10.** 1.6 m =   **11.** 2.2 m =   **12.** 7.6 m =

Hint:
2 m = 200 cm
4.2 m = 420 cm

Exercise 7

Change these centimetre measurements into metre measurements.

1. 100 cm =   **2.** 200 cm =   **3.** 500 cm =   **4.** 700 cm =
5. 900 cm =   **6.** 800 cm =   **7.** 400 cm =   **8.** 750 cm =
9. 420 cm =   **10.** 160 cm =   **11.** 370 cm =   **12.** 50 cm =

Hint:
100 cm = 1 m
750 cm = 7.5 m

†World records for sizes of animals.
1: 10 m long; 2: 16 m long; 3: 6 m tall;
4: 33.5 m long; 5: 26.5 m long; 6: 1.0 m long.

MEASUREMENTS IN KILOMETRES

You use kilometres to measure large distances.

The world's highest mountain is Everest. It stands about 9 km above sea level.

The deepest part of the ocean is called Challenger Deep. It is about 11 km deep.

9 km

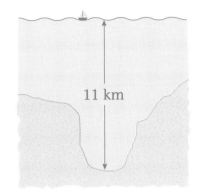

11 km

Remember: There are 1000 metres in a kilometre.
1 km = 1000 m or 1000 m = 1 km

Exercise 8

Change these kilometre measurements into metre measurements.
  1. 2 km =   **2.** 5 km =   **3.** 9 km =   **4.** 1.5 km =
  5. 3.5 km =   **6.** 0.5 km =   **7.** 3.2 km =   **8.** 8.1 km =

Exercise 9

Change these metre measurements into kilometre measurements.
  1. 3000 m =   **2.** 8000 m =   **3.** 1000 m =   **4.** 6000 m =
  5. 4500 m =   **6.** 7500 m =   **7.** 1200 m =   **8.** 3400 m =

  9. One lap of a running track is 400 m.
      James runs 10 laps of the track. How many kilometres has he run?
10. These electricity pylons are 200 m apart.
      There are 5 cables attached to each pylon.

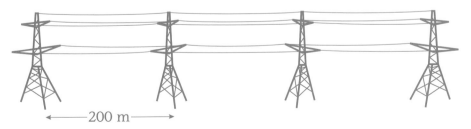

←—— 200 m ——→

  a How many metres of cable are needed to connect these four pylons?
  b Convert this distance into kilometres.

REVIEW 2

S W3IV3Я

A. COORDINATES

Give the coordinates for the letters
marked on the grid.

1. *a* is at (___ , ___)
2. *b* is at (___ , ___)
3. *c* is at (___ , ___)
4. *d* is at (___ , ___)
5. *e* is at (___ , ___)
6. *f* is at (___ , ___)

What do you find at these coordinates?

7. (2,4) =
8. (9,1) =
9. (1,9) =
10. (10,6) =

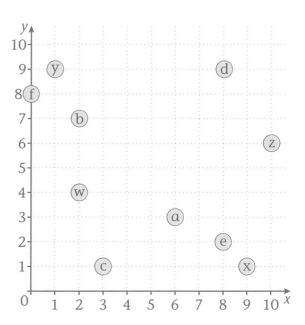

B. CODES

1. Use this code to find out what
   message is written below.

   4,5,9   2,6,4,4,3

   3,5,2,2,6,8   2,6,4,4,3

e = 5	o = 6	y = 3
d = 9	r = 4	
l = 2	w = 8	

2. Here is a code that uses coordinates.
   Look at the grid on the right.
   Each of the coordinates below
   will give you a letter on the grid.

   (2,4)   (9,5)   (7,2)   (1,1)
   (5,3)   (5,6)   (0,2)   (8,0)
   (2,3)   (9,3)   (10,2)
   (6,1)   (9,3)   (7,2)   (0,2)
   (6,1)   (3,5)   (7,4)   (10,6)   (4,1)

   Can you read the message?

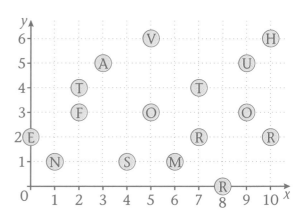

C. ANGLES

Remember there are 180° in a straight angle.
Find the missing angle.

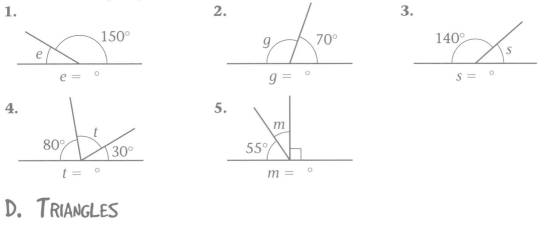

1.

150°

e

e =   °

2.

g   70°

g =   °

3.

140°   s

s =   °

4.

80°   t   30°

t =   °

5.

55°   m

m =   °

D. TRIANGLES

Remember there are 180° in a triangle.
Find the missing angle.

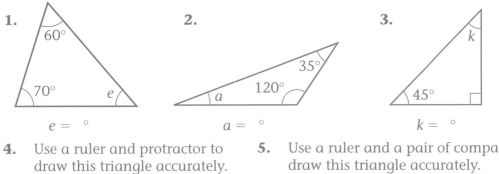

1.

60°

70°   e

e =   °

2.

35°

120°   a

a =   °

3.

k

45°

k =   °

4. Use a ruler and protractor to draw this triangle accurately.

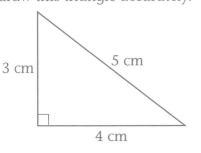

3 cm   5 cm

4 cm

5. Use a ruler and a pair of compasses to draw this triangle accurately.

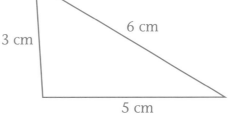

3 cm   6 cm

5 cm

E. PROBLEMS

1. How much greater is 50 than 35?
2. How many 10p pieces are there in £1.20?
3. Put these units of measurement in order of size, beginning with the smallest: metre; millimetre; kilometre; centimetre.
4. Put these numbers in order of size, beginning with the smallest: 251; 189; 991; 1001; 300.
5. If one minibus holds 15 people, how many would 4 minibuses hold?

F. Time

1. An aircraft takes off from Gatwick at 1 p.m. It lands in Paris at 2.17 p.m. How long does the journey take?
2. A train leaves Glasgow at 7.30 a.m. It arrives in Birmingham at 11.45 a.m. How long does the journey take?
3. A ferry leaves Dover at 11 a.m. and arrives in Calais at 1.15 p.m. How long does the journey take?
4. Jenny takes 15 minutes to write one page of work. How long would it take her to write six pages?
5. A bus arrives at the bus stop once every ten minutes. How many buses would arrive in one hour?

Look at these bus times. They are given in 24-hour time.

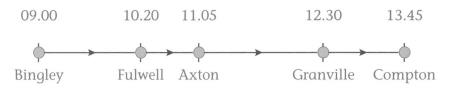

| 09.00 | 10.20 | 11.05 | 12.30 | 13.45 |

Bingley   Fulwell   Axton   Granville   Compton

Write down how long the journey takes:

6. from Bingley to Fulwell
7. from Fulwell to Axton
8. from Axton to Granville
9. from Fulwell to Compton.
10. How long does the total journey take?

G. Distance

1. Use the scale on the right to find the height of:
   a the gas holder
   b the TV tower
   c Nell's Store
   d the Airways Building
   e the Weston Bank
2. What is the difference in height between Nell's Store and the Weston Bank?
3. What is the difference in height between the Weston Bank and the gas holder?
4. What is the difference in height between the TV tower and the Airways Building?
5. What is the difference in height between Nell's Store and the TV tower?

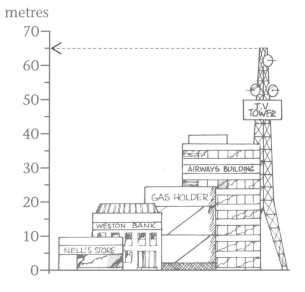

H. FRACTIONS

1. What is $\frac{1}{2}$ of 16?   **2.** What is $\frac{1}{4}$ of 12?   **3.** What is $\frac{1}{3}$ of 9?

4. What is $\frac{1}{2}$ of 20?   **5.** What is $\frac{1}{5}$ of 20?   **6.** What is $\frac{1}{4}$ of 16?

7. What is $\frac{3}{4}$ of 8?   **8.** What is $\frac{2}{3}$ of 15?   **9.** What is $\frac{2}{5}$ of 15?

10. Which is bigger, $\frac{1}{2}$ of 18 or $\frac{1}{4}$ of 20?

11. Which is bigger, $\frac{1}{2}$ of 12 or $\frac{1}{3}$ of 30?

12. Which of these fractions is the same as $\frac{1}{2}$? $\frac{2}{8}, \frac{2}{4}, \frac{5}{10}, \frac{3}{7}$

I. CIRCLES

1. The radius of each small circle is 2 cm.
   What will be the diameter of the large circle?

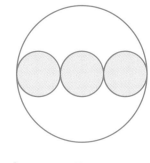

2. This round pond has a diameter of 5 metres.
   A fountain is placed in the centre of the pond.
   The fountain has a diameter of 1 metre.
   How far will the fountain be from the edge
   of the pond?

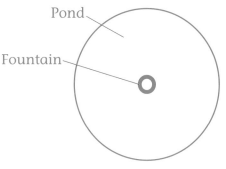

Pond

Fountain

J. NUMBER

Do these problems in your head. See how many you can do in 5 minutes.

Addition

  1. $4 + 5 =$ **2.** $3 + 7 =$ **3.** $6 + 8 =$ **4.** $10 + 8 =$

  5. $17 + 6 =$ **6.** $20 + 13 =$ **7.** $19 + 23 =$ **8.** $25 + 27 =$

Subtraction

  9. $9 - 5 =$ **10.** $12 - 4 =$ **11.** $15 - 6 =$ **12.** $18 - 10 =$

13. $22 - 18 =$ **14.** $21 - 7 =$ **15.** $32 - 13 =$ **16.** $43 - 26 =$

Multiplication

17. $2 \times 4 =$ **18.** $3 \times 3 =$ **19.** $8 \times 2 =$ **20.** $4 \times 4 =$

21. $6 \times 5 =$ **22.** $4 \times 10 =$ **23.** $5 \times 8 =$ **24.** $12 \times 4 =$

Division

25. $6 \div 2 =$ **26.** $8 \div 4 =$ **27.** $10 \div 2 =$ **28.** $10 \div 5 =$

29. $12 \div 4 =$ **30.** $20 \div 5 =$ **31.** $30 \div 6 =$ **32.** $42 \div 7 =$

11 GRAPHS

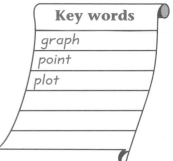

Key words

graph

point

plot

This unit will help you to:
→ **read graphs**
→ **use graphs to display information clearly.**

READING GRAPHS

Graphs are used to display information so that it can be clearly understood.
The wall shows Toby's height every year.

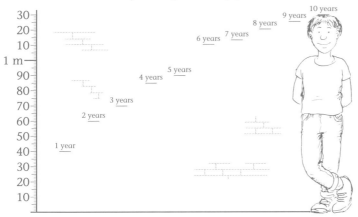

This information can be easily
displayed on a graph.

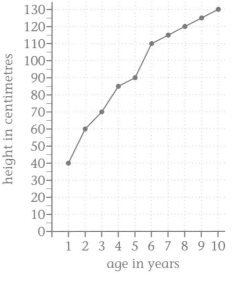

Exercise 1

1. How tall was Toby when he was
   a one year old   **b** six years old   **c** five years old
   d four years old   **e** nine years old   **f** ten years old?
2. How old was Toby when he was   **a** 70 cm tall   **b** 115 cm tall?
3. How much did Toby grow between   **a** years 1 and 2   **b** years 5 and 6?

Pauline is doing a project on the human heart.
She wants to know if the heart beat changes after exercising.
She does 'step-ups' on a stool for one minute.
She then sits down and takes her pulse rate every minute. Here are the results.

	Number of heart beats
In the 1st minute	120
In the 2nd minute	90
In the 3rd minute	85
In the 4th minute	75
In the 5th minute	70

The graph shows how Pauline's pulse rate changed during 5 minutes.

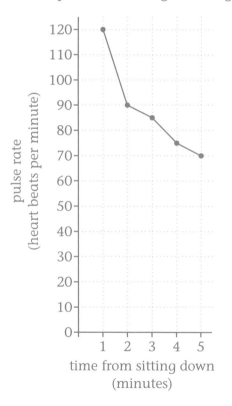

Exercise 2

1. What is the highest number of heart beats on the graph?
2. What is Pauline's pulse rate after 2 min?
3. What is her pulse rate after 4 min?
4. What is her pulse rate after 3 min?
5. How long is it until her pulse rate drops to 70 beats per min?

Exercise 3

Roy is saving some of his pocket money. He uses the graph to record his savings.

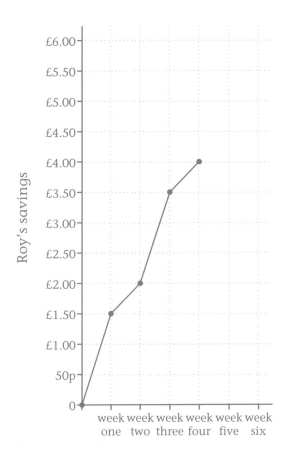

1. How much did he save during week one?

2. How much had he saved by week two?

3. How much had he saved by week three?

4. How much had he saved by week four?

5. How much did he add to his savings between week two and week three?

6. How much did he add to his savings between week three and week four?

7. Roy saved 50p in week five, so his total savings were £4.50. Copy the graph above and plot this point.

8. His aunt gave him £1.00 in week six. He then had £5.50. Plot this point on your graph.

Exercise 4

This graph shows the temperatures that have been recorded between 10 a.m. and 6 p.m. The temperature is taken every hour and measured in degrees Celsius (°C).

1. What is the **highest** temperature recorded?
2. What is the **lowest** temperature recorded?
3. What is the temperature at 12 noon?
4. What is the temperature at 4 p.m.?
5. At what times is the temperature 14°C?
6. At what times is the temperature 9°C?
7. How many degrees does the temperature **rise** between 11 a.m. and 2 p.m.?
8. How many degrees does the temperature **fall** between 4 p.m. and 6 p.m.?

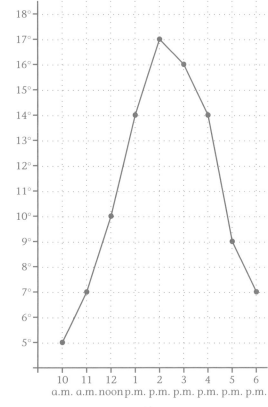

Exercise 5

1. Copy the grid on the right. Use cm squared paper.
2. Plot the points for these temperatures and times.

    | 10 a.m. | → | 9°C |
    | 11 a.m. | → | 9°C |
    | 12 noon | → | 10°C |
    | 1 p.m. | → | 12°C |
    | 2 p.m. | → | 13°C |
    | 3 p.m. | → | 11°C |
    | 4 p.m. | → | 9°C |
    | 5 p.m. | → | 8°C |
    | 6 p.m. | → | 5°C |

3. Join these points to complete your graph.

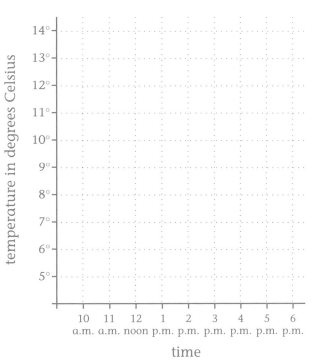

12 TIME AND DISTANCE

Key words

kilometre

speed

distance

This unit will help you to:
→ **link time, distance and speed**
→ **read and draw time and distance graphs.**

DISTANCE ON A MAP

Exercise 1

The Speedee Delivery van carries goods from Westport to local shops.
Here is the map that the driver uses.

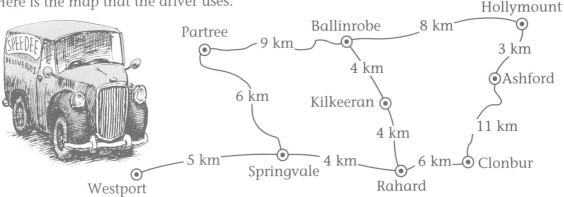

Use the map to answer these questions:
1. Springvale is ____ kilometres from Clonbur.
2. Partree is ____ kilometres from Westport.
3. Clonbur is ____ kilometres from Hollymount.
4. The van goes from Westport to Springvale, Rahard and Kilkeeran. How far has it travelled?
5. From Kilkeeran the van goes to Ballinrobe, Hollymount and Ashford. How far has it travelled?
6. From Ashford the van goes to Hollymount, Ballinrobe and Partree. How far is this journey?
7. How far is it from Rahard to Hollymount by the shortest route?
8. How far is it from Partree to Ashford by the shortest route?
9. Give directions for a journey from Springvale to Hollymount.
10. Make a drawing of these signs and fill in the missing information.
    a The signpost in Kilkeeran   **b** The signpost in Ashford

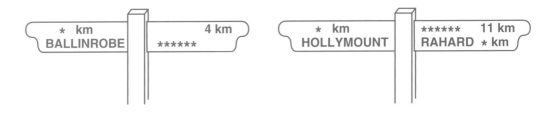

Exercise 2

Jo entered the Cresswell car rally.
The diagram shows her start-time at A, the time at each check-point,
and the time at the finish F.

1. How long did she take for each stage?
   a A to B   **b** B to C   **c** C to D
   d D to E   **e** E to F
2. How long did the first two stages take?
3. How long did the last three stages take?
4. What was the total time taken from start to finish?
5. Which stage took the shortest time?

Exercise 3

Jo takes part in another rally. The rally starts at P and finishes at V.

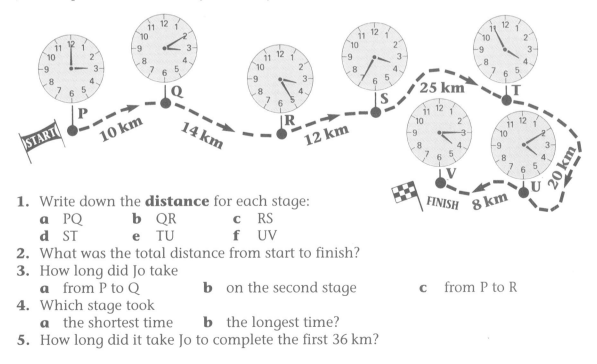

1. Write down the **distance** for each stage:
   a PQ   **b** QR   **c** RS
   d ST   **e** TU   **f** UV
2. What was the total distance from start to finish?
3. How long did Jo take
   a from P to Q   **b** on the second stage   **c** from P to R
4. Which stage took
   a the shortest time   **b** the longest time?
5. How long did it take Jo to complete the first 36 km?

TRAVEL GRAPHS

A good way to show the time and distance travelled on a journey is on a travel graph.

Time is shown horizontally. Distance is shown vertically.

Exercise 4

This graph shows a rally car travelling from A to G.

Check-points A to G show the distance and time from the start.

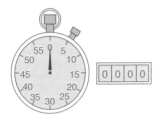

The stop-watch and the trip-meter start when the car starts.

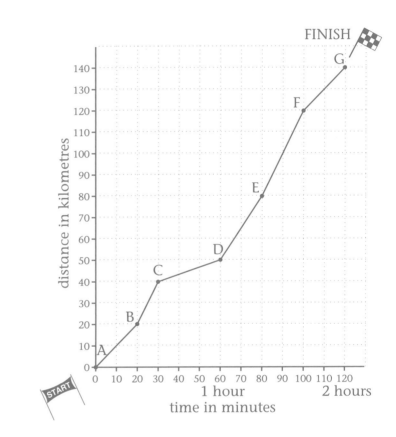

1. How long did the car take to reach check-point B?
2. What was the distance from check-point A to check-point B?
3. How far has the car travelled between check-points A and C?
4. How long did the car take to travel from A to D?
5. How far did the car travel between C and E?
6. How far did the car travel in the first hour?
7. Which check-point did the car reach in the first 80 minutes?
8. How long did it take to reach check-point F?
9. How many kilometres did the car travel between check-points C and G?
10. How many kilometres was the total journey?
11. How many hours did the total journey take?
12. How long did it take the car to travel from:
    a A to B?   **b** B to C?   **c** C to D?   **d** D to E?   **e** E to F?   **f** F to G?

Exercise 5

This travel graph is incomplete.
The graph should show a
journey from A to F.
The data required to complete
the graph is given in the table.

Stage of journey	Distance of stage	Time taken
from A to B	2 kilometres	10 minutes
from B to C	3 kilometres	20 minutes
from C to D	1 kilometre	5 minutes
from D to E	5 kilometres	20 minutes
from E to F	3 kilometres	15 minutes
Totals	14 kilometres	70 minutes

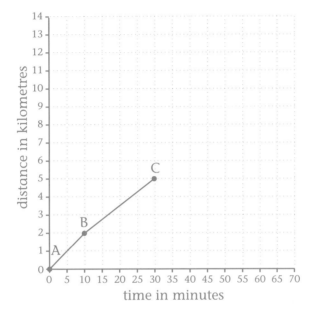

1. Copy the graph on cm squared paper.
2. Study the table and then complete the graph. Label each stage of the journey. The next stage goes from C to D.
3. Write down the type of transport that you think made the journey.
   a The Concorde airliner   **b** A bicycle
   c A sports car   **d** A high-speed train

Exercise 6

Rosie went for a cycle ride. She measured the time and distance travelled for each stage of her ride.
Here are her results:

- Rosie cycled the first 6 km in 10 minutes.
- She took 30 minutes to cycle the next 4 km.
- Rosie cycled the next 5 km in 20 minutes.
- She finished her cycle ride 30 minutes later after cycling another 3 km.

1. Make a table similar to the one in Exercise 5.
2. Draw a graph to show Rosie's journey.

Exercise 7

Here is a map of a train journey from Penzance to London.
The train leaves Penzance at 10.00 a.m. and arrives in London at 3.00 p.m.

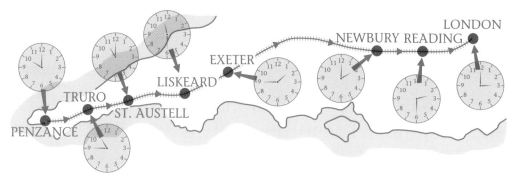

The distance between each station is shown below in kilometres.

The travel graph for the journey is shown below; it is incomplete.

1. Make a table showing the distance between each station and the time taken to travel between each station.

2. Copy the graph below onto grid paper.

3. Complete the graph showing each station in the correct place. The first three stations have been marked for you.

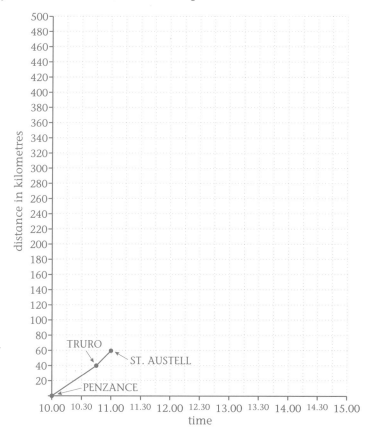

Barry goes for a walk. Here is a graph of his journey.

He walks a total of 3 miles in one hour.

After 30 minutes, he stops for a rest. The rest lasts 10 minutes.

When Barry is resting, the distance remains the same, but time still keeps ticking by …

Exercise 8

These travel graphs show three different journeys.

a

b

c

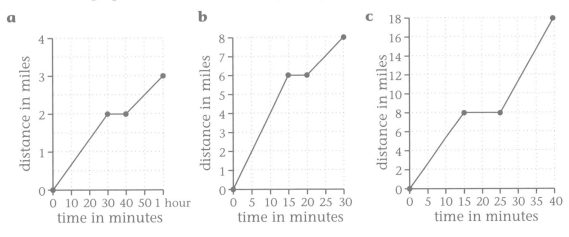

Answer these questions for each graph.
1. What distance was the journey?
2. How much time did it take?
3. How long did the stop last for?
4. What distance had been travelled before the stop?
5. How much time had passed before the stop?

Exercise 9

Here is the travel graph of Pam's cycle ride.
1. How long did the first 4 miles take?
2. How far had Pam cycled in the first 25 minutes?
3. How much time passed before the first stop?
4. How many minutes did Pam rest for at Point A?
5. Which was the longest stop: A, B or C?
6. How long was the longest stop?
7. When did Pam stop to rest at point C?
8. For how long did Pam cycle between stops A and B?

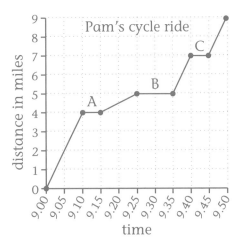

13 THE FOUR RULES 2

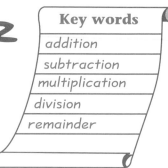

Key words

addition

subtraction

multiplication

division

remainder

This unit will help you to:

→ **decide on appropriate number operation**

→ **divide and find remainders**

→ **improve addition skills**

→ **multiply by 10.**

Exercise 1

For these problems, four calculations are shown.
Only one of the calculations leads to the correct answer.
Find the correct calculation and solve the problem.

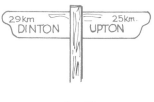

1. From the signpost it is 29 km to Dinton and 25 km
to Upton. How far is it from Dinton to Upton?
   a $25 - 29$ **b** $29 + 25$ **c** $29 - 25$ **d** $25\overline{)29}$

2. Mr Webb plants 4 rows of daffodils with 8 bulbs in each
row. How many bulbs has he planted?
   a $8 + 4$ **b** $8 - 4$ **c** $8 \div 4$ **d** 4×8

3. If Mr Webb had to plant 48 bulbs, how many rows would
he need to plant if he still wanted 8 bulbs in a row?
   a 48×8 **b** $48 \div 8$ **c** $48 + 8$ **d** $48 - 8$

4. There were 67 people on the bus. After the bus stopped,
there were 29 people left on board. How many people
got off the bus?
   a $67 - 29$ **b** $67 + 29$ **c** $29 - 67$ **d** $67 \div 29$

5. The train is 262 m long. If 77 m is out of the tunnel, how
much is still inside?
   a $262 + 77$ **b** $77 + 262$ **c** $77 - 262$ **d** $262 - 77$

6. In the Rex Cinema there are seats for 96 people. How
many rows are there if there are 8 seats in each row?
   a $96 \div 8$ **b** 96×8 **c** $96 - 8$ **d** $8 + 96$

7. If 237 queued to watch the film at the Rex Cinema,
how many would not be allowed in the cinema?
   a 96×237 **b** $237 - 96$ **c** $237 + 96$ **d** $96 + 237$

8. The cinema was rebuilt. It now has 9 rows with 25 seats
in each row. How many people will the cinema hold?
   a $25 + 9$ **b** $25 \div 9$ **c** 25×9 **d** $9 + 25$

DIVISION AND REMAINDERS

Farmer Jones' hen has laid 13 eggs.
He puts the eggs into cartons.
Each carton holds 6 eggs.
He fills 2 cartons but there is 1 egg left over.

Numbers that are left over in division
are called **remainders**.

Exercise 2

These eggs are packed in cartons in groups of six.
Find the remainder of eggs left over in these questions.

1. 7 eggs	**2.** 9 eggs	**3.** 15 eggs	**4.** 21 eggs
5. 25 eggs	**6.** 32 eggs	**7.** 19 eggs	**8.** 35 eggs
9. 12 eggs	**10.** 29 eggs	**11.** 43 eggs	**12.** 23 eggs

Example 1

Cakes are packed in their boxes
in groups of 10.

Number of cakes	Boxes filled	Cakes left over over (remainder)
22	2	2

If the baker makes 22 cakes:

How many boxes will he fill?
How many cakes will be left over?

He will fill two boxes and there will be
2 cakes left over.

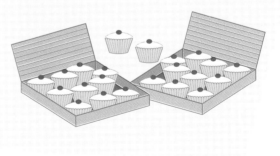

Exercise 3

Draw a table like the one in the example. In your table write down:

- The number of cakes.
- The number of boxes filled.
- The number of cakes left over.

1. 25 cakes	**2.** 31 cakes	**3.** 17 cakes	**4.** 45 cakes
5. 39 cakes	**6.** 57 cakes	**7.** 40 cakes	**8.** 88 cakes
9. 92 cakes	**10.** 107 cakes	**11.** 135 cakes	**12.** 216 cakes

Example 2

These cakes are packed in boxes
in groups of 5.

If the baker makes 12 cakes, how many boxes
will he use?

How many cakes will be left over?

He will use two boxes and 2 cakes will
be left over.

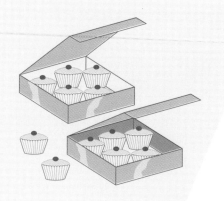

Exercise 4

Write down

• the number of boxes used
• the number of cakes left over

for each of these questions.
Write your answers in a table
as shown.

	No. of cakes	Boxes	Remainder
1.	11	2	1
2.			
3.			

1. 11 cakes	**2.** 16 cakes	**3.** 8 cakes	**4.** 13 cakes
5. 18 cakes	**6.** 19 cakes	**7.** 22 cakes	**8.** 33 cakes
9. 40 cakes	**10.** 47 cakes	**11.** 56 cakes	**12.** 64 cakes

Exercise 5

The baker now uses boxes that hold 8 cakes each.
Write down

• the number of boxes used
• the number of the remainder

for each question. Write your answer in a table as before.

1. 9 cakes	**2.** 12 cakes	**3.** 15 cakes	**4.** 17 cakes	**5.** 20 cakes
6. 27 cakes	**7.** 42 cakes	**8.** 36 cakes	**9.** 55 cakes	**10.** 48 cakes

Exercise 6

Answer these division problems.
There will be a remainder each time.

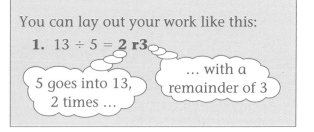

You can lay out your work like this:

1. $13 \div 5 = $ **2 r3**

5 goes into 13, 2 times …

… with a remainder of 3

1. $13 \div 5 =$	**2.** $11 \div 2 =$	**3.** $13 \div 3 =$	**4.** $17 \div 4 =$	**5.** $14 \div 6 =$
6. $19 \div 4 =$	**7.** $18 \div 5 =$	**8.** $20 \div 3 =$	**9.** $28 \div 5 =$	**10.** $40 \div 3 =$
11. $45 \div 10 =$	**12.** $26 \div 6 =$	**13.** $27 \div 7 =$	**14.** $31 \div 6 =$	**15.** $78 \div 10 =$

WRITTEN PROBLEMS

Work out these problems in your head.
How many on each card can you do in 10 minutes?

Workcard 1

1. What is 2, add 3, add 7?
2. What is 20 take away 5?
3. What is 10 times 6?
4. What will 20 shared by 4 come to?
5. What total do you get if you add 12 to 8?
6. Take 8 from 20.
7. What is 11 multiplied by 4?
8. How many times does 6 go into 30?
9. Add 6, 4 and 11.
10. What is 5 times 11?

Workcard 2

1. What is 6, add 10, add 12?
2. Take 8 from 25.
3. What will 7 times 5 make?
4. What is 18 divided by 2?
5. Add 7, 4, 11 and 9.
6. What is the difference between 19 and 41?
7. What is 12 multiplied by 5?
8. What is 50 divided by 5?
9. What is 31, take away 26?
10. Share 18 into 9 groups. How many in each group?

Workcard 3

1. Add 23 to 17?
2. What is the difference between 31 and 13?
3. Multiply 13 by 5.
4. What will 25 shared by 5 come to?
5. What is 91 plus 11?
6. What is 54 minus 28?
7. What do you get if you multiply 4 by 17?
8. What is 120 divided by 10?
9. Add 24 and 25 and 26.
10. What is 17 multiplied by 5?

Workcard 4

1. What is 10, add 20, add 32?
2. What is 105 minus 26?
3. What is 10 multiplied by 10?
4. What is 35 divided by 7?
5. What is the total when you add 195 to 36?
6. Find the difference between 38 and 106.
7. Multiply 23 by 6.
8. Divide 8 into 88.
9. Take 48 away from 110.
10. Share 64 by 8.

MULTIPLYING BY 10

This is Base 10 equipment.

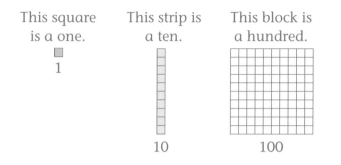

This square
is a one.

1

This strip is
a ten.

10

This block is
a hundred.

100

Exercise 7

Write the number represented by the shapes.
The first one is done for you.

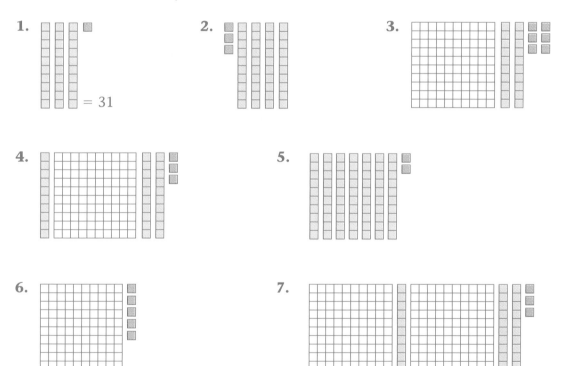

1. = 31

2.

3.

4.

5.

6.

7.

Exercise 8

Use drawings like the ones above to show these numbers.

1. 27   **2.** 74   **3.** 35   **4.** 309
5. 3 × 2   **6.** 4 × 2   **7.** 3 × 3   **8.** 2 × 5

Example 3

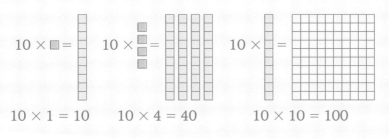

$10 \times 1 = 10$ $10 \times 4 = 40$ $10 \times 10 = 100$

Exercise 9

Draw the numbers which are 10 times bigger than these.

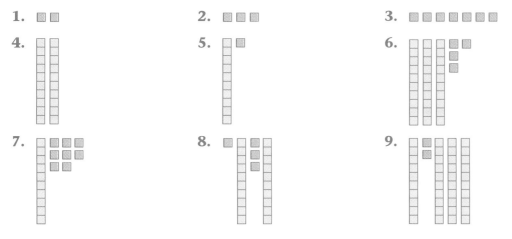

10. Now write out in your book a multiplication statement for each of the drawings above, like this: **1.** $10 \times 2 = 20$

Look at your answers to question **10.**

There is a pattern in the answers.
$$10 \times 2 = 20$$
$$10 \times 7 = 70$$
$$10 \times 11 = 110$$

When a number is multiplied by 10, you can see that

- the units move to the tens column,
- the tens move to the hundreds column, and so on,
- you put a nought at the end of the number.

Exercise 10

Multiply these numbers by 10.

1. 9	**2.** 12	**3.** 15	**4.** 19	**5.** 20	**6.** 21
7. 27	**8.** 30	**9.** 35	**10.** 39	**11.** 41	**12.** 63

14 NUMBER PATTERNS

This unit will help you to:
→ **find simple number patterns involving factors, prime numbers and square numbers.**

TABLES PRACTICE

Exercise 1
Write down the answers to these problems.

1. $6 \times 2 =$ **2.** $2 \times 6 =$ **3.** $5 \times 4 =$

4. $2 \times 7 =$ **5.** $8 \times 3 =$ **6.** $3 \times 4 =$

7. $8 \times 10 =$ **8.** $7 \times 5 =$ **9.** $7 \times 3 =$

10. $3 \times 9 =$ **11.** $10 \times 5 =$ **12.** $6 \times 9 =$

Example 1

This is a multiplication table for numbers 1 to 10.

This square shows $3 \times 4 = 12$

This square shows $7 \times 2 = 14$

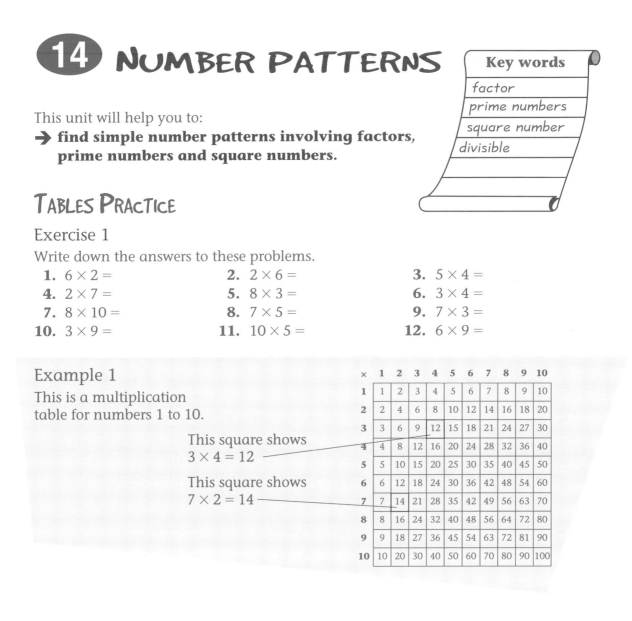

×	1	2	3	4	5	6	7	8	9	10
1	1	2	3	4	5	6	7	8	9	10
2	2	4	6	8	10	12	14	16	18	20
3	3	6	9	12	15	18	21	24	27	30
4	4	8	12	16	20	24	28	32	36	40
5	5	10	15	20	25	30	35	40	45	50
6	6	12	18	24	30	36	42	48	54	60
7	7	14	21	28	35	42	49	56	63	70
8	8	16	24	32	40	48	56	64	72	80
9	9	18	27	36	45	54	63	72	81	90
10	10	20	30	40	50	60	70	80	90	100

Exercise 2
Use the table to answer these questions.

1. $9 \times 7 =$ **2.** $8 \times 8 =$ **3.** $5 \times 9 =$

4. $8 \times 7 =$ **5.** $10 \times 9 =$ **6.** $7 \times 7 =$

7. $6 \times 10 =$ **8** $8 \times 9 =$ **9.** $5 \times 8 =$

10. $9 \times 9 =$ **11.** $10 \times 10 =$ **12.** $7 \times 8 =$

Exercise 3
Copy these statements.
Use the table to say whether they are true or false.

1. $4 \times 5 = 5 \times 4$ **2.** $7 \times 6 = 6 \times 7$ **3.** $4 \times 4 = 2 \times 8$

4. $3 \times 9 = 7 \times 4$ **5.** $2 \times 2 \times 5 = 2 \times 10$ **6.** $4 \times 2 \times 5 = 2 \times 3 \times 7$

Activity   FACTORS

Cut a shape like this
from a piece of card

Put this shape over the multiplication
table (page 106) like this.
The number in the corner is 12
so, 12 = 3 × 4.

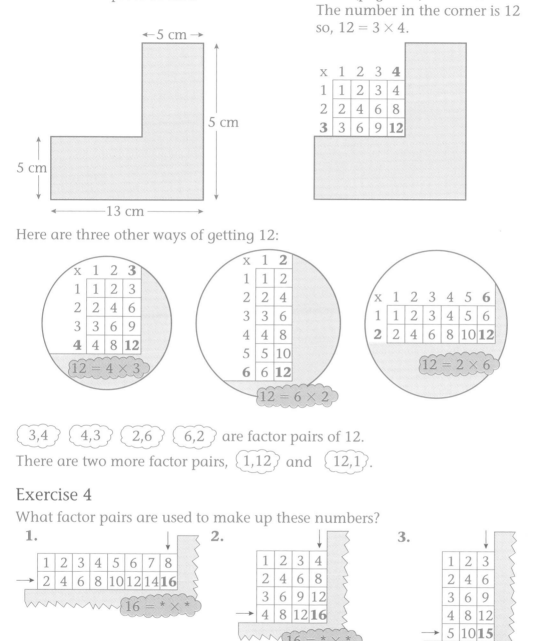

Here are three other ways of getting 12:

$12 = 4 \times 3$ $12 = 6 \times 2$ $12 = 2 \times 6$

3,4   4,3   2,6   6,2   are factor pairs of 12.

There are two more factor pairs, 1,12 and 12,1.

Exercise 4

What factor pairs are used to make up these numbers?

1.

1	2	3	4	5	6	7	8
2	4	6	8	10	12	14	**16**

16 = * × *

2.

1	2	3	4
2	4	6	8
3	6	9	12
4	8	12	**16**

16 = * × *

3.

1	2	3
2	4	6
3	6	9
4	8	12
5	10	**15**

15 = * × *

4. Find four factor pairs for 10.   **5.** Find some factor pairs for 15.
6. Find some factor pairs for 21.   **7.** Find some factor pairs for 8.
8. Find some factor pairs for each of the following numbers:
    a 24   **b** 9   **c** 25   **d** 36   **e** 16   **f** 40

FACTOR TREES

Example 2
This is a factor tree for 24. Watch how it grows.

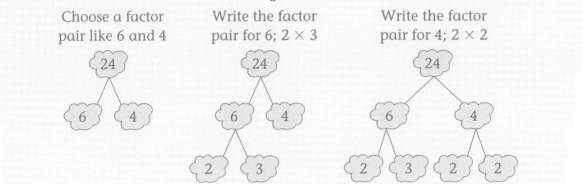

Exercise 5
Copy and complete these factor trees.

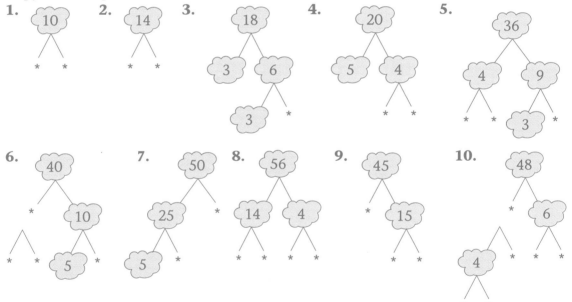

This is the last line of the factor tree for 24.

The tree stops here because these numbers can only be divided by one or themselves. If the tree was continued, it would go on for ever.

Exercise 6
Copy and complete these factor trees as far as you can.

DIVISIBILITY

The numbers 4, 8, 12, 16, 20, 24, . . . are all in the 4 times table.
These numbers are all divisible by 4. This means that 4 divides into these numbers without leaving a remainder.

Notice that 6 does not appear in the 4 times table. This is because 6 is not divisible by 4; 6 ÷ 4 is 1 with a remainder of 2.

×	1	2	3	4	5	6	7	8	9	10
1	1	2	3	4	5	6	7	8	9	10
2	2	4	6	8	10	12	14	16	18	20
3	3	6	9	12	15	18	21	24	27	30
4	4	8	12	16	20	24	28	32	36	40
5	5	10	15	20	25	30	35	40	45	50
6	6	12	18	24	30	36	42	48	54	60
7	7	14	21	28	35	42	49	56	63	70
8	8	16	24	32	40	48	56	64	72	80
9	9	18	27	36	45	54	63	72	81	90
10	10	20	30	40	50	60	70	80	90	100

Exercise 7

Copy the part of the multiplication table shown below.
Three extra boxes have been added to each row. Fill in the extra boxes.

		8	9	10	11	12	13
1	...	8	9	10			
2	...	16	18	20			
3	...	24	27	30			
4	...	32	36	40	44	48	52
5	...	40	45	50			
6	...	48	54	60			
7	...	56	63	70			
8	...	64	72	80			
9	...	72	81	90			
10	...	80	90	100			

Exercise 8

Answer these questions.

1. Is 22 divisible by 2?
2. Is 45 divisible by 9?
3. Is 63 divisible by 7?
4. Is 57 divisible by 7?
5. Is 42 divisible by 5?
6. Is 27 divisible by 2?
7. Is 60 divisible by 5?
8. Is 96 divisible by 8?
9. Is 78 divisible by 7?
10. Is 25 divisible by 3?
11. Is 117 divisible by 9?
12. Is 39 divisible by 3?

PRIME NUMBERS

There are 10 pupils in class 2T. They each have their own desk.
Here are their ten desks.

The desks could be arranged like this:

    2 rows of 5 desks

Exercise 9
Draw three different ways of arranging these desks in equal rows or columns.

1. 10 desks   **2.** 18 desks   **3.** 15 desks   **4.** 20 desks

   If there are 5 desks you could only
arrange them in two ways:

1 row of 5 desks   or   5 rows of 1 desk

There are only 2 ways of arranging the desks because 5 is only
divisible by 1 and itself.

5 has only one factor pair (1, 5) (or (5, 1) which is the same thing).

A number which is only divisible by 1 and itself is called a **prime number**.

Exercise 10
In each list of numbers, say which number is the prime number.

1. 4,6,3,9,12   **2.** 2,4,8,10,15   **3.** 6,3,16,14,4
4. 4,8,10,7,9   **5.** 8,6,9,12,11   **6.** 13,15,20,25,30

Square numbers

The first square number is 1.

The second square number is 4.

The third square number is 9.

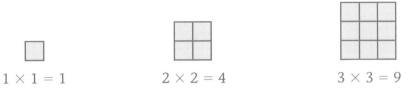

$1 \times 1 = 1$ $2 \times 2 = 4$ $3 \times 3 = 9$

Exercise 11

Draw the next three square numbers on squared paper. Write a sentence for each drawing like the sentences above.

Exercise 12

In the times table the shaded boxes show the first 3 square numbers.

1. Make a list of all the square numbers from 1 to 100.
2. Work out the next two square numbers after 100.

×	1	2	3	4	5	6	7	8	9	10
1	1	2	3	4	5	6	7	8	9	10
2	2	4	6	8	10	12	14	16	18	20
3	3	6	9	12	15	18	21	24	27	30
4	4	8	12	16	20	24	28	32	36	40
5	5	10	15	20	25	30	35	40	45	50
6	6	12	18	24	30	36	42	48	54	60
7	7	14	21	28	35	42	49	56	63	70
8	8	16	24	32	40	48	56	64	72	80
9	9	18	27	36	45	54	63	72	81	90
10	10	20	30	40	50	60	70	80	90	100

REVIEW 3

A. SHAPE

One of these dolls contains diamonds. Use the clues below to decide which one.

The diamond-filled doll has a round nose.
The diamond-filled doll has a square head.
The diamond-filled doll has a rectangular mouth.
The diamond-filled doll has triangles on its tie. Which doll is it?

B. GRAPHS

This graph shows the temperature during the course of one day, between 9 o'clock in the morning and 6 o'clock in the evening.

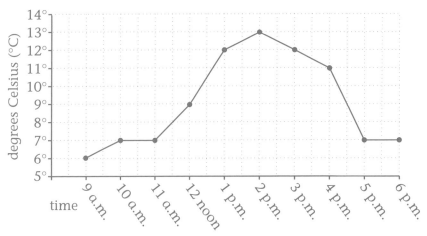

1. What was the temperature at 12 noon?
2. What was the temperature at 4 p.m.?
3. What was the temperature at 9 a.m.?
4. At what time did the temperature reach 13°C?
5. On two occasions the temperature reached 12°C. At what times did this occur?
6. How many degrees did the temperature drop between:
   a 2 p.m. and 3 p.m.   **b.** 3 p.m. and 4 p.m.   **c.** 4 p.m. and 5 p.m.?

C. FRACTIONS

1. If you gave away half of the eight chocolates in the box, how many would you have left?
2. How many chocolates are there in a quarter of the box?
3. One half of the chocolates is the same as ____ quarters or $\frac{1}{2} = \frac{*}{4}$
4. Copy and complete each pair of equivalent fractions.

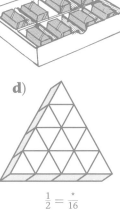

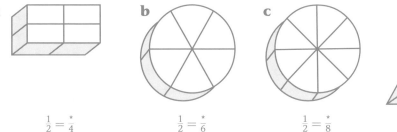

a $\frac{1}{2} = \frac{*}{4}$ b $\frac{1}{2} = \frac{*}{6}$ c $\frac{1}{2} = \frac{*}{8}$ d) $\frac{1}{2} = \frac{*}{16}$

D. POSITION

Look at the map. Imagine you are standing at **X** facing the railway bridge.

1. What is the first road on the left?
2. How many turnings on the right is Finlay St?
3. There are two bridges on the map. In which streets are the bridges?
4. Which is the second street on the left?
5. The school is found at the junction of two roads; which roads are they?
6. Write down the directions to the railway station.
7. Write down the directions to the car park.
8. Imagine that you are standing at the car park. Write down the directions to the church.
9. Imagine that you are standing by the school in Disraeli Terrace. Write down the directions to the car park going by Pit St.
10. Imagine that you are standing by the Police Station in Copper Rd. Write down the directions to Walton St by going along Pit St.

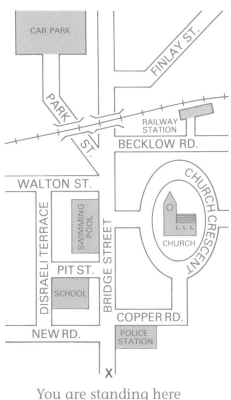

You are standing here facing the railway bridge.

E. TRIANGLES

1. Copy out these three sentences and fill in the missing words.
   a   The sides of an equilateral triangle are all the ____ length.
   b   An isosceles triangle has ____ sides of the same length.
   c   The three sides of a scalene triangle are all ____.

2. Copy and complete the table. Say whether the triangles are scalene, isosceles or equilateral.

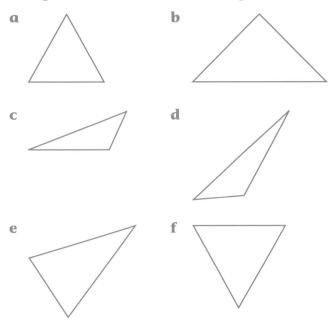

Triangle	Type
a	equilateral
b	
c	
d	
e	
f	

3. Use a ruler and a pair of compasses to construct triangles with these sides.
   a   4 cm, 5 cm, 3 cm.
   b   5.5 cm, 4.5 cm, 7.5 cm
   c   3.6 cm, 4.7 cm, 6.1 cm

F. CODES

A	B	C	D	E	F	G	H	I
20	6	11	16	22	30	8	17	5

J	K	L	M	N	O	P	Q
46	4	12	27	15	9	14	24

R	S	T	U	V	W	X	Y	Z
40	7	13	4	2	23	29	10	19

Use the information above to put these messages into code.
Code each letter like this: A (2 × 10) or A (16 + 4) or A (5 × 4), etc.

a   MATHS IS FUN   **b**   I LIKE TEACHERS

G. COORDINATES

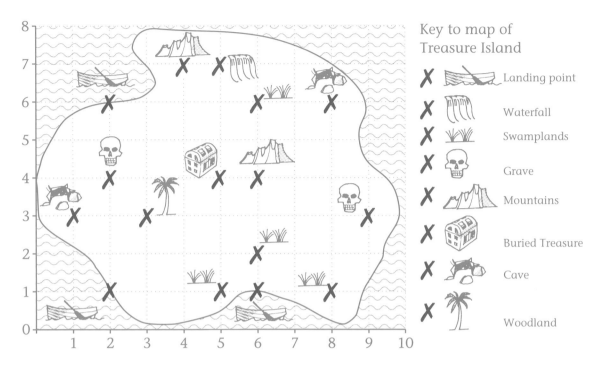

Use the key to help you answer these questions about the map.
1. Where are the three landing points?
2. What can be found at (3,3)?
3. Where would you go to drink fresh water?
4. What are the positions of the four swamps?
5. What will you see at (4,7) and (6,4)?
6. How many graves are there on the island?
7. What are the positions of the graves?
8. Where will you find the two caves?
9. Write down the coordinates of four places in the sea.
10. Where could you find buried treasure?

H. TIME

Match the time on each digital clock with the correct clock time.

 15 STREET MATHS I

THE YOUTH CLUB

Exercise 1

Here is a bar chart showing attendances at the Youth Club for one week.

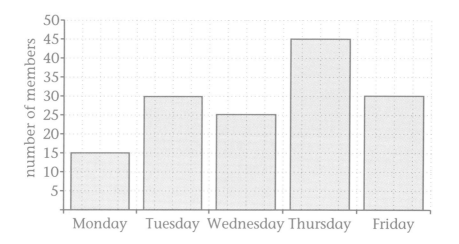

1. How many members attended on:
   a Monday   **b** Tuesday   **c** Wednesday   **d** Thursday   **e** Friday?
2. Each member pays 50p to attend . How much money was collected on:
   a Monday   **b** Tuesday   **c** Wednesday   **d** Thursday   **e** Friday?
3. How much money was collected during the week altogether?

Exercise 2

The Youth Club are designing a new membership card.
The card must have the following things written on it.

Warren View Youth Club   *Name*

Membership number   *Address*

Draw a rectangle the same size as the one here.
Design a new membership card.
Decorate it with patterns and geometric shapes.

Membership card

6 cm

7 cm

THE YOUTH CLUB COMPETITION

NUMERACY

It is competition night at the Youth Club.
There are four events in the competition: table tennis
darts
cards
snooker

Six people take part in the competition.

Here is how they did in the four events.

Table tennis	Darts	Cards	Snooker
1st Mary	1st Sally	1st Leroy	1st Leroy
2nd Carlos	2nd Mary	2nd Jan	2nd Sally
3rd Sally	3rd Carlos	3rd Sally	3rd Carlos
4th Leroy	4th Leroy	4th Mary	4th Sam
5th Jan	5th Sam	5th Carlos	5th Mary
6th Sam	6th Jan	6th Sam	6th Jan

Here is the points table

1st	= 8 points
2nd	= 7 points
3rd	= 5 points
4th	= 3 points
5th	= 2 points
6th	= 1 points

Exercise 3

Copy and complete this results table.

Name	Total score	Position
Jan		
Leroy		
Mary		
Sally		
Sam		
Carlos		

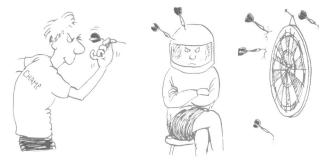

THE YOUTH CLUB CANTEEN

This is Mrs Bright. She runs the Youth Club canteen.
Here is the canteen price list.

Tea	25p
Coffee	45p
Cola	50p
Biscuits	22p
Chews	18p
Crisps	25p
Roll	90p

Exercise 4

How much have these members spent in the canteen?
1. Sally bought a cup of coffee and a bag of crisps.
2. Leroy bought a can of cola and two biscuits.
3. Mary bought a cup of tea, a bag of crisps and a chew.
4. Tom bought two cups of tea and a roll.
5. Jan bought two cans of cola and two bags of crisps.

Profits
6. If the Youth Club make 4p profit on every bag of crisps sold, how much profit
   would they make on **a** 6 bags **b** 20 bags **c** 12 bags?
7. If the Youth Club make 7p profit on every can of cola sold, how much profit
   would they make on **a** 4 cans **b** 10 cans **c** 8 cans?

Exercise 5

Mrs Bright keeps a cash book.
In her cash book she writes down
each night how much money she
takes (income).
She also writes down on the day the
money that she spends (expenses).
A page from her cash book is opposite.

1. Copy the page of her cash book
   neatly and complete it.
2. What was the total income for
   the week?
3. What were the total expenses for
   the week?
4. What was the total profit (income
   minus expenses)?

	Income	Expenses
Mon.	£14.45	£15.28
Tues.	£16.22	—
Wed.	£13.10	£10.56
Thur.	£20.03	£10.60
Fri.	£22.25	—

YOUTH CLUB FUND RAISING

Exercise 6

The Youth Club needs a new minibus.
To raise the money, the members decide to organise a sponsored swim.
Here are the sponsorship forms of three club members.

Name _Rob_
Lengths completed _6_

Sponsor	Amount per length	Total
Mr King	20p	£1.20
Mrs Singh	£1.00	
Mary Stern	10p	
Billy	25p	
Ms Ellis	50p	

Name _Nazim_
Lengths completed _10_

Sponsor	Amount per length	Total
Mrs Allen	50p	
B Unice	30p	
Mr Kelly	10p	
Jamie Gordon	25p	
Charlotte	40p	
Ms Greg	£1.00	
Mr Siad	90p	

Name _Tyrone_
Lengths completed _9_

Sponsor	Amount per length	Total
Sally Joe	10p	
Miss Wallis	£1.00	
Mr Crow	50p	
Mrs Crow	20p	
Tom Dean	£2.00	
N Ahmed	60p	
Ms McBain	30p	

Copy and complete each form.
1. How much money did Rob raise?
2. How much money did Nazim raise?
3. How much money did Tyrone raise?
4. How much did the three of them raise together?

Exercise 7

Here is another sponsorship form. Copy and complete it.

Name _Jenny_
Lengths completed _8_

Sponsor	Amount per length	Total
B Brown	50p	?
S Smith	?	£4.00
Gill	?	£8.00
Mr Khan	30p	?
Mrs Khan	?	80p
Miss Clegg	?	£2.40p

THE YOUTH CLUB TRIP

Exercise 8

The Youth Club are going camping for the weekend.
Here is the map of the journey to the camp site.

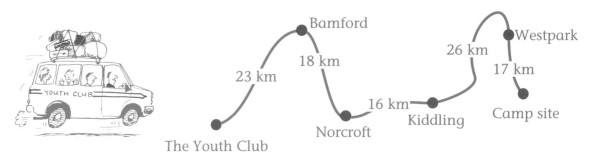

1. How many kilometres is it from the Youth Club to Norcroft?
2. How many kilometres is it from Bamford to Westpark?
3. How many kilometres is the journey from the Youth Club to the camp site?
4. If the minibus travels 50 kilometres in one hour, how long will the whole journey take?
5. If the minibus travels 10 kilometres on one litre of petrol, how many litres of petrol will the minibus use on the journey?

Exercise 9

The cost of staying at the camp site is £1.50 a night for each person.
To park the minibus costs £2.00 a night.
There are 11 Youth Club members, camping for two nights.

1. What is the cost for 11 people camping for one night?
2. What is the cost of camping **and** parking for one night?
3. What is the total cost of camping for two nights?
4. What is the total cost of camping **and** parking for two nights?
5. The bill for camping and parking is paid for with a £50 note. How much change should there be?

Exercise 10

During the weekend the party go walking.
They divide into two groups, group A and group B.
Below is a map of the walks that the two groups take.

(map with the following locations and distances:)
The Old Mill — 8½ km — Horseshoe Lake — 3km
Scott's Hill — 4½ km — Denton Church — Camp Site
Group B — Horseshoe Lake — 3½ km — Bovis Castle
5km — Scott's Hill
Group A
4km — Camp Site
Cox Wood — 4km
Fender Bridge — 6½ km — Cobb's Cave — 5½ km — Bovis Castle
4km — Cobb's Cave

1. How far is it to walk from the camp to:
   a Horseshoe Lake   **b** Scott's Hill   **c** Fender Bridge
2. How far does Group A walk?
3. How far does Group B walk?

Exercise 11

Before the group return home they buy some presents.
Work out how much money each person spent.

1. Clare's presents

Paperweight £4.50
Key ring £1.75
Cobb's Cave

2. Ali's presents

Mug £3.25
Bovis Castle
Toy £3.80
Fudge £2.00

3. James's presents

Each stick of rock costs 55p
Picture £8.00

4. Shaun's presents

Glass £1.99
Brian's Glass
Music box £11.20
Pencil case £2.60

 **16 AREA**

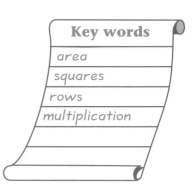

Key words

area

squares

rows

multiplication

This unit will help you to:

→ **understand what area is**

→ **know how area is measured and calculated**

→ **improve your multiplication skills.**

Mr Gadbury is fed-up with cutting the grass.

He puts 5 slabs in a line.

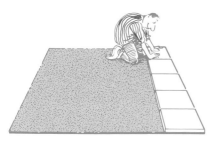

The **area** of the lawn is **25 squares**.
Remember that area is counted in **squares**.

He decides to cover the lawn with square slabs.

He needs 5 lines of slabs, so he uses 25 of them.

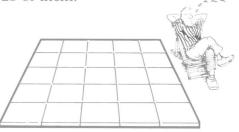

Exercise 1

What is the area covered by the square slabs?
Write your answers like this: 'The area is . . . . squares.'

1.

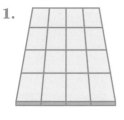

2.

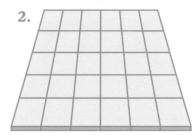

3.

Exercise 2

Each of these lawns has been paved with square tiles. Count the squares to find the area of each one. Write this sentence for each of your answers: 'The area of the lawn is . . . . squares.'

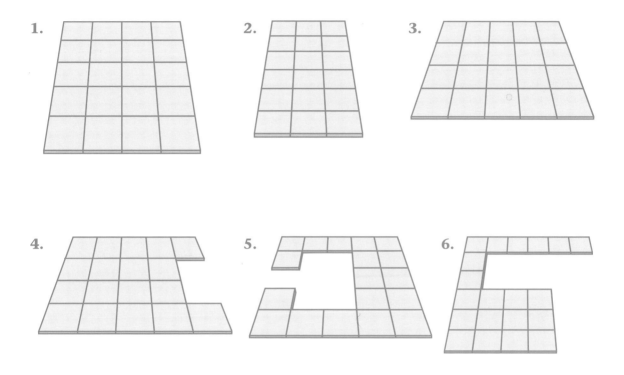

1.

2.

3.

4.

5.

6.

In questions **7** to **10**, give an estimate of the areas covered by:

- counting the whole squares
- counting the part squares that are a half or bigger.

Write your answers like this: 'The area of the garden is about . . . . squares.'

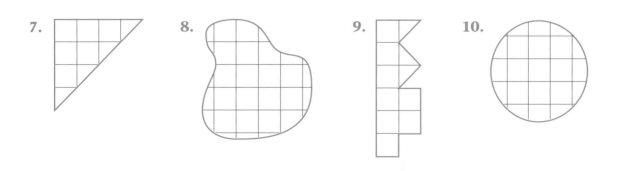

7.

8.

9.

10.

AREA AND MULTIPLICATION

Example 1

Each row of this rectangle has 5 squares in it.
There are 4 rows.
Altogether there are **'4 lots of 5 squares'**;
20 squares.

So you can find the area of the rectangle by
multiplying: **5 × 4 = 20 squares**.

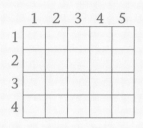

Exercise 3

Find the area of the rectangles and squares below. The first one is done for you.

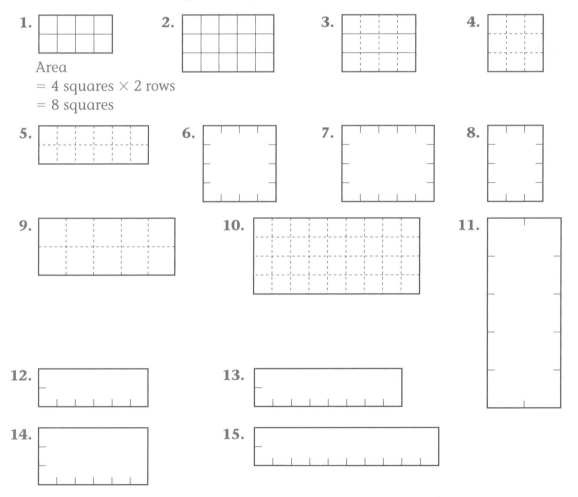

1.

Area
= 4 squares × 2 rows
= 8 squares

2.

3.

4.

5.

6.

7.

8.

9.

10.

11.

12.

13.

14.

15.

Rows

Mr Gadbury has 12 tiles left over. He can arrange the tiles into different rectangles. Each rectangle has an area of 12 squares.

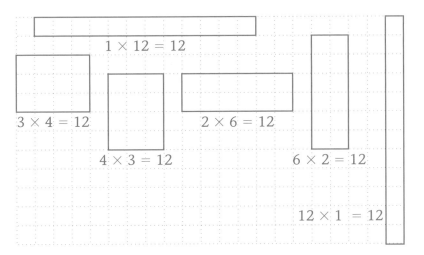

$1 \times 12 = 12$

$3 \times 4 = 12$

$4 \times 3 = 12$

$2 \times 6 = 12$

$6 \times 2 = 12$

$12 \times 1 = 12$

Exercise 4

Rearrange these groups of tiles into squares or rectangles .

- Draw your answers on squared paper.
- Write a multiplication showing the number of tiles in each row, and the number of rows.

Find as many arrangements as you can.

Hint:
Use counters to help you.

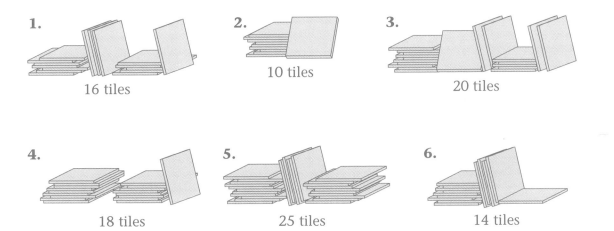

1.

16 tiles

2.

10 tiles

3.

20 tiles

4.

18 tiles

5.

25 tiles

6.

14 tiles

STANDARD MEASUREMENTS

Mr Gadbury could have used any square tile.
If he wanted to tell some one about the area of his
garden they would be confused, because squares
can be any size.

You use **standard squares**, so that everyone can
tell whether an area is large or small.

You use **centimetre squares (cm²)**
for small areas like the area of the top
of a match box.

You use **metre squares (m²)** for
larger areas like the area covered by a
carpet in your classroom.

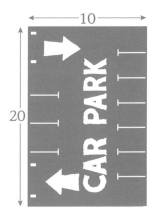

Exercise 5

1. Look at each drawing below; their units are missing
(cm or m). Decide whether the areas of the items should
be measured in **centimetre squares** or **metre
squares** (**cm²** or **m²**).

The drawings are not
drawn to size, do not
try to measure them.

a

5
4

b

DIARY

5
8
R.J.A

c

10

CAR PARK

20

d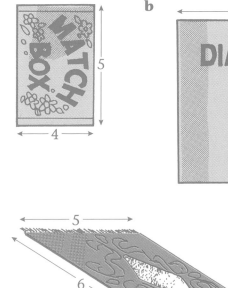

5
6

e

10

Makeup
Box

10

f

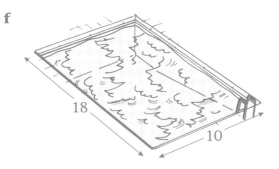

18
10

g

Toothpaste

11
3

h

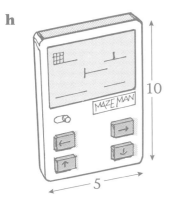

MAZE MAN

10
5

i

2
1

j

PENCIL BOX

4
15

k

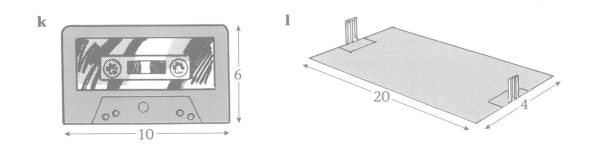

6
10

l

20
4

2. Calculate the area of each of these items above.
Show your multiplication like this: **a**   Area = 5 cm × 4 cm
                    = 20 cm²

COMPLEX SHAPES

Example 2

Mr Gadbury has made this 'T' shaped path from square tiles. You can find the area of the path by counting. Its area is 14 squares.

If the path was much bigger, it would take you too long to count, and you could easily make a mistake.

You can **calculate** the area of the shape if you imagine that it is made out of 2 rectangles.

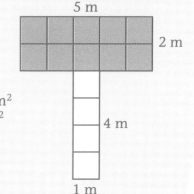

- The area of the orange rectangle $= 5\,\text{m} \times 2\,\text{m} = 10\,\text{m}^2$
- The area of the white rectangle $\;= 1\,\text{m} \times 4\,\text{m} = 4\,\text{m}^2$
- To get the total area of the path you add the two smaller areas together.
  $10\,\text{m}^2 + 4\,\text{m}^2 = 14\,\text{m}^2$

Exercise 6

1. Calculate the area of the sections of paths below. They are all measured in m^2.

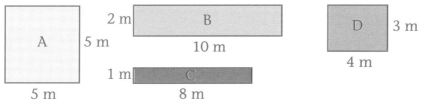

2. These garden paths are made from the lettered sections above. Find their areas.

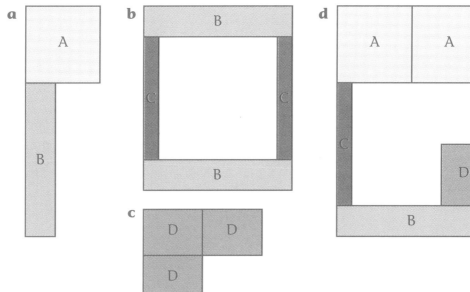

AREAS AND ROWS

Example 3

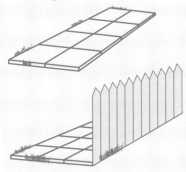

This path has an area of 8 m². It is made from **2 rows**. Each row is made from 4 tiles.

This path has an area of 15 m². There are 3 rows, but you cannot see how many square tiles there are in each row.

There must be 5 squares in a row because 3 rows of 5 makes 15.

You can work it out two ways: $3 \times \boxed{5} = 15$
                                  or $15 \div 3 = \boxed{5}$

Exercise 7

1. Find the number of rows.

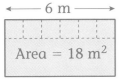

6 m

Area = 18 m²

2. How many tiles in each row?

5 m

Area = 20 m²

3. How many tiles in each row?

4 m

Area = 40 m²

4. Find the number of rows.

10 m

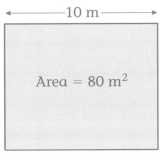

Area = 80 m²

5. Find the number of rows.

20 m

Area = 60 m²

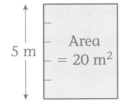

6. Find the number of rows.

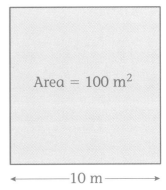

Area = 100 m²

10 m

 SHAPE

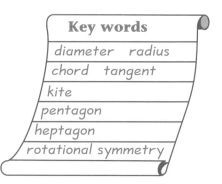

Key words

diameter   radius

chord   tangent

kite

pentagon

heptagon

rotational symmetry

This unit will help you to:
→ **identify and describe 2D shapes**
→ **know the parts of a circle**
→ **identify and find order of rotational symmetry.**

RADIUS AND DIAMETER

Remember: In a circle the **radius** is the distance from the centre to the edge.

The **diameter** is the distance all the way across through the centre.

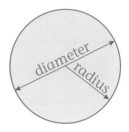

Exercise 1

Find the radius of each of these objects.

1. The radius of the tyre is ____ cm.

2. The radius of the dial is ____ cm.

Exercise 2

Copy and complete the sentences below.
The questions are about the drawings above.

1. The diameter of the dial is ____ cm.

2. The diameter of the tyre is ____ cm.

Exercise 3

Copy and complete the table.

Radius	Diameter
5 cm	?
$2\frac{1}{2}$ cm	?
7 cm	?
?	20 cm
?	30 cm

LINES AND CIRCLES

The centre of each circle is marked O.

The lines marked *a*, *b* and *c* are called **chords**.

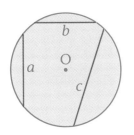

The lines marked *d*, *e* and *f* are called **tangents**.

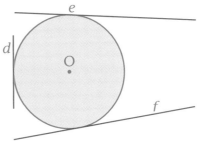

Chords touch the circle in two places.

Tangents touch the circle in only one place.

Exercise 4

Copy and complete the sentences below.

1. The centre of the circle is marked with the letter ____.
2. The line marked *r* is the _____ of the circle.
3. Lines *x* and *y* are called _____.
4. The shortest chord is line ____.

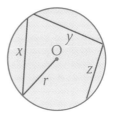

Exercise 5

Copy and complete the sentences below.

1. The line *j* is called the _____.
2. The lines *h* and *n* are called _____.
3. The line *k* is called a _____.
4. The lines *p* and *m* are called _____.

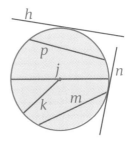

Exercise 6

Measure each line, then copy and complete the sentences below.

1. The radius is ____ cm long.
2. The tangent line is ____ cm long.
3. The shortest chord is ____ cm long.
4. The diameter is ____ cm long.

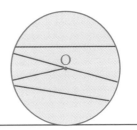

Polygons

Any closed shape with straight sides is a polygon.
You should know these polygons.

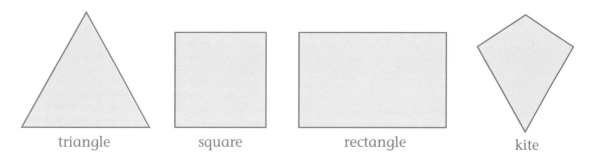

triangle   square   rectangle   kite

These shapes are called regular polygons.

pentagon   hexagon   heptagon   octagon
5 sides   6 sides   7 sides   8 sides

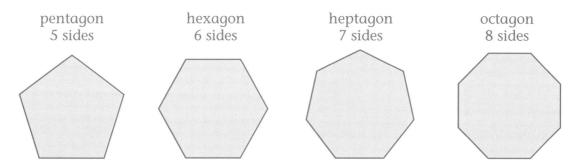

A regular polygon has sides that are all the same length.
A regular polygon has angles that are all the same size.

Exercise 7

Name these polygons.

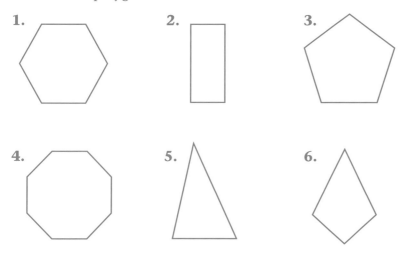

1.   2.   3.

4.   5.   6.

Exercise 8

Put these shapes through the sorter. See where they come out.

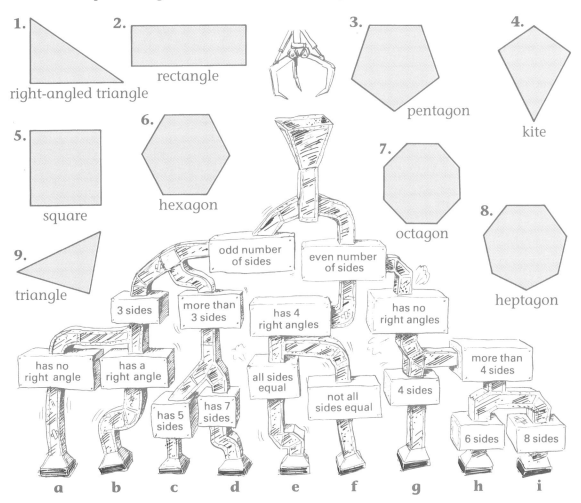

1. right-angled triangle
2. rectangle
3. pentagon
4. kite
5. square
6. hexagon
7. octagon
8. heptagon
9. triangle

Copy and complete this table for each shape.

Shape number	Where does it come out	Description			Name
1	b	odd number of sides	3 sides	has a right angle	right-angled triangle

SYMMETRY

Turn this page upside down.
What do you notice about this word?

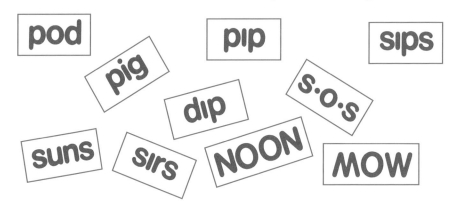

Even when you turn the word upside down, it
still looks the same and it still reads 'chump'.

Exercise 9

Which of the words below look the same when they are turned upside down?

pod   pig   pip   dip   s.o.s   sips   suns   sirs   NOON   MOW

In one whole turn (one rotation) the word chump looks the same twice.

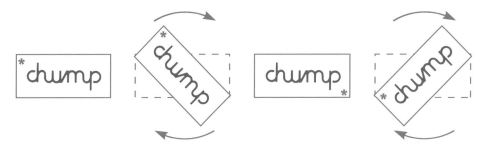

It has a **rotational symmetry of order 2**.

This shape looks the same three times (at **b**, **d**, and **f**) in one rotation.

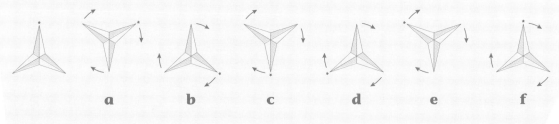

a   b   c   d   e   f

The shape has a rotational symmetry of order 3.

Exercise 10

Copy and complete the table giving the rotational order of these shapes.
It may help if you trace each shape and then turn it round.

a

b

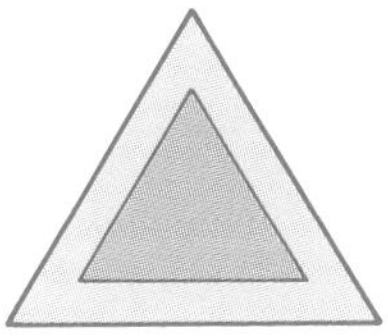

c

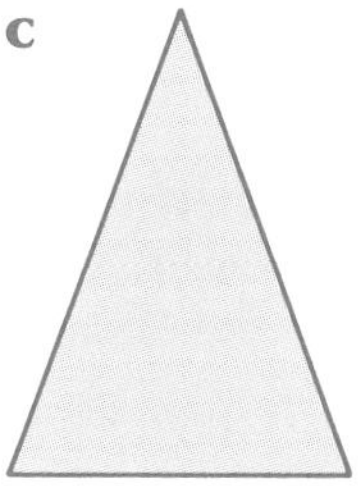

Shape	Rotational order
a	2
b	
c	1
d	
e	
f	
g	
h	
i	
j	
k	
l	
m	4
n	
p	
q	
r	
s	
t	
u	

d

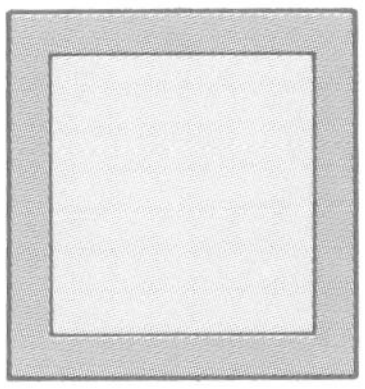

e

f

g

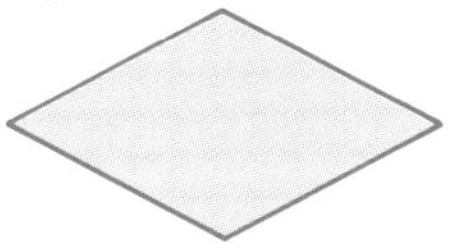

h

i

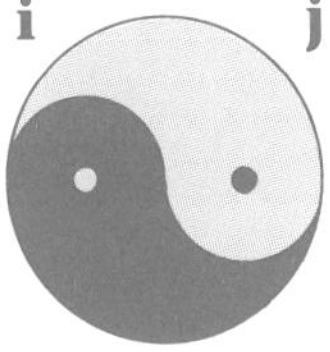

j

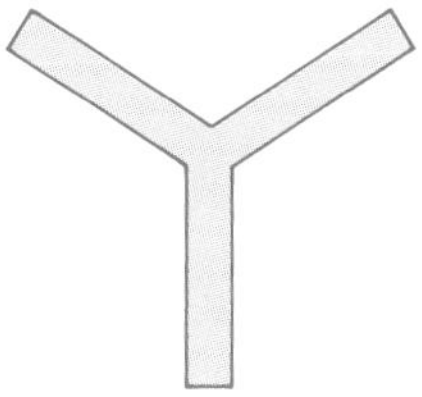

k

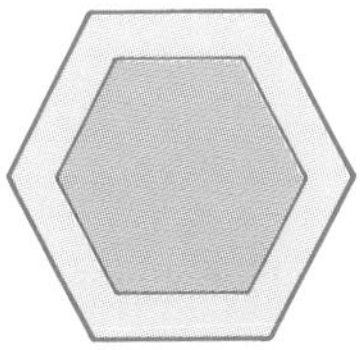

l

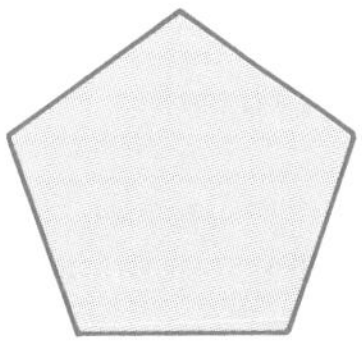

m

n

p

q

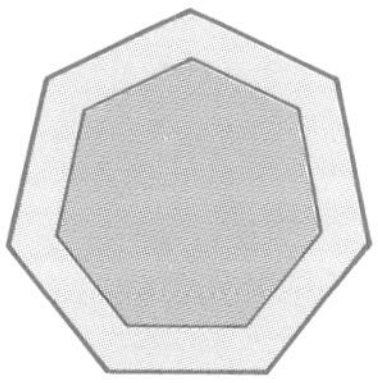

r

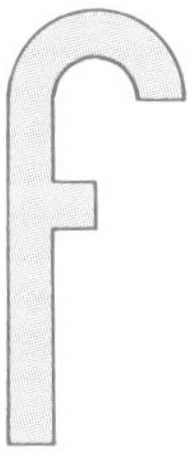

s

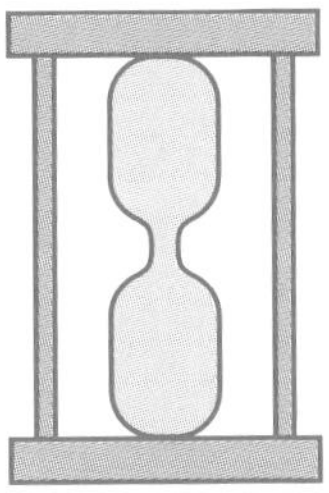

t

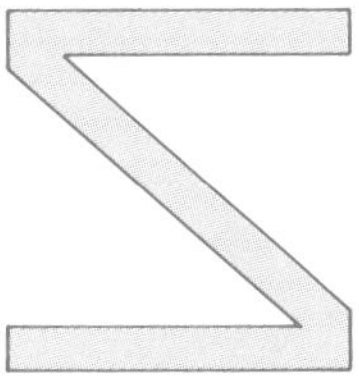

u

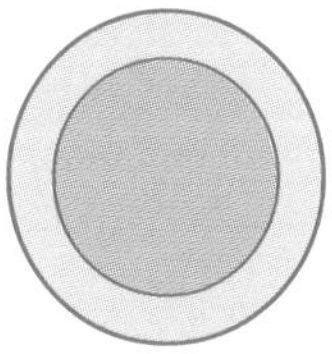

18 ALGEBRA

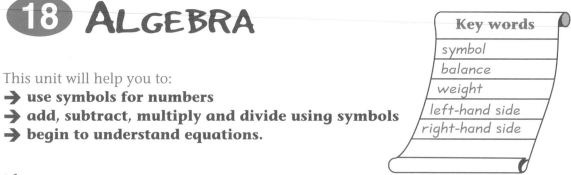

Key words

| symbol |
| balance |
| weight |
| left-hand side |
| right-hand side |

This unit will help you to:
→ **use symbols for numbers**
→ **add, subtract, multiply and divide using symbols**
→ **begin to understand equations.**

USING SYMBOLS

Symbols can represent information, ideas, and also numbers.

This symbol represents one pound in money.

This symbol represents poison.

This symbol represents ladies.

Exercise 1

Each symbol below gives some information.
Write down the meaning of each and where you might find it.

1.   **2.**   **3.**   **4.**

5. "999"   **6.**   **7.**   **8.** DANGER

Exercise 2

Draw your own symbols to represent these ideas.

1. No shouting   **2.** This is a classroom   **3.** No teachers allowed
4. Dining room   **5.** Your own name   **6.** Fairground

WORKING WITH SYMBOLS

In algebra, symbols usually represent objects or numbers. You need to know how to deal with symbols in maths.

Example 1

In one hand, there is one apple. In the other, there are two apples. Altogether there are 3 apples.

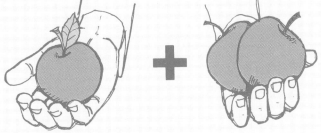

If you use the symbol *a* for apple, you can write the sum like this: $a + 2a = 3a$
The symbol *a* was chosen because the word apple starts with *a*; but you could use any symbol you like.

Exercise 3

Write out a sum for each box and give the answer. Use symbols not words. The first one is done for you.

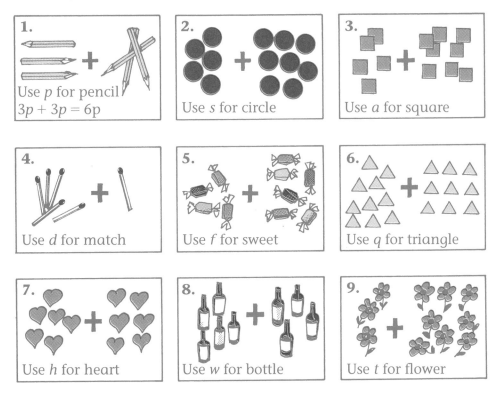

1.
Use *p* for pencil
$3p + 3p = 6p$

2.
Use *s* for circle

3.
Use *a* for square

4.
Use *d* for match

5.
Use *f* for sweet

6.
Use *q* for triangle

7.
Use *h* for heart

8.
Use *w* for bottle

9.
Use *t* for flower

Exercise 4

Simplify these problems using symbols.

Here is an example:
$5a - 2a = 3a$

1. $6a - 4a =$ **2.** $10p - 8p =$ **3.** $17x - 10x =$
4. $11a - 8a =$ **5.** $12b - 6b =$ **6.** $21e - 10e =$
7. $22d - 5d =$ **8.** $30q - 20q =$ **9.** $32m - 20m =$
10. $50s - 25s =$ **11.** $50x - 28x =$ **12.** $60t - 25t =$

Exercise 5

Add up these symbols. Be careful to add all of the symbols.

Here is an example:
$a + 2a + 4a = 7a$

1. $b + 5b + 6b =$ **2.** $10a + 3a + 2a =$ **3.** $4s + 3s + 7s =$
4. $9p + 20p + 8p =$ **5.** $14p + 20p + p =$ **6.** $t + 2t + t + 5t =$
7. $a + 5a + 16a =$ **8.** $15x + 5x + 16x =$ **9.** $26a + a + 2a + 3a =$
10. $q + 7q + 10q + q =$ **11.** $2m + 3m + 2m + 10m =$ **12.** $15z + 12z + z + z =$

Example 2

Here are 2 apples and 3 bananas.
If you add the two quantities, you would not
say that you had 5 'banapples'.

You can only add symbols that are *alike*.

You can only combine '*a*' with '*a*' and '*b*' with
'*b*', etc.

a for apple
b for banana
$2a + 3b$ is **not** $5ab$

Exercise 6

Add up the like symbols in these problems.

Here is an example: $2a + 3a + 3b + b = 5a + 4b$

1. $a + 2a + 3b =$ **2.** $2a + 5a + 4b + 2b =$ **3.** $6p + 2t + 5p + 4t =$
4. $4s + s + 3r + s =$ **5.** $5q + p + 2p + 6q =$ **6.** $10p + 4q + q + 2q =$
7. $3x + 2y + x + 5y =$ **8.** $10a + 2c + a + 3c =$ **9.** $7f + g + 3g + 3f =$
10. $h + h + 5h + 2j =$ **11.** $2s + 5s + x + s =$ **12.** $4k + 6y + k + 3y =$
13. $5x + x + t + 8t =$ **14.** $4e + 8c + 5e + c =$ **15.** $e + e + t + 9e + t =$

BALANCING PROBLEMS

Example 3

The two sides of the scales balance: they are equal in weight.

To find out how much each box marked x weighs:

Two x's weigh 10
So one x weighs 5

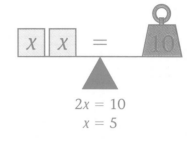

$2x = 10$
$x = 5$

Exercise 7

Find the weight of the objects marked x.

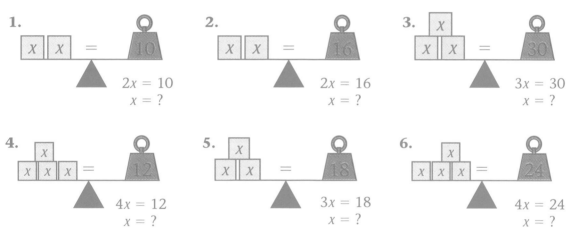

1. $2x = 10$
$x = ?$

2. $2x = 16$
$x = ?$

3. $3x = 30$
$x = ?$

4. $4x = 12$
$x = ?$

5. $3x = 18$
$x = ?$

6. $4x = 24$
$x = ?$

Exercise 8

Calculate the weight of one box. In each question the boxes are the same weight.

1. Three boxes weigh 6 kg.
2. Five boxes weigh 20 kg.
3. Ten boxes weigh 30 kg.
4. Four boxes weigh 40 kg.
5. Six boxes weigh 18 kg.
6. Five boxes weigh 30 kg.

Exercise 9

Find the value of x in each problem below.

1. $2x = 20$
2. $3x = 30$
3. $3x = 6$
4. $3x = 15$
5. $2x = 40$
6. $3x = 45$
7. $5x = 20$
8. $5x = 15$
9. $4x = 16$
10. $3x = 27$
11. $6x = 30$
12. $6x = 48$

Example 4

In this problem, there are *x*s on both sides of the balance.

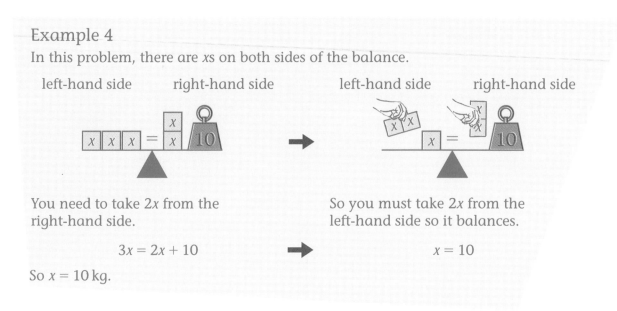

You need to take 2*x* from the right-hand side.

$$3x = 2x + 10$$

So you must take 2*x* from the left-hand side so it balances.

$$x = 10$$

So *x* = 10 kg.

Exercise 10

Find the value or 'weight' of *x* in each problem.

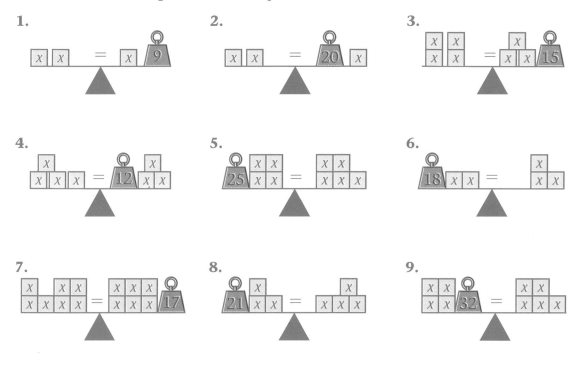

Exercise 11

Find the value or 'weight' of *x* in each problem.

1. $3x = 2x + 10$ 2. $5x = 4x + 12$ 3. $2x + 6 = 3x$
4. $7x + 1 = 8x$ 5. $12x + 9 = 13x$ 6. $25 + 15x = 16x$

Example 5

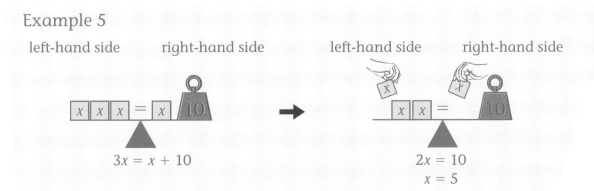

left-hand side   right-hand side   left-hand side   right-hand side

$3x = x + 10$ $2x = 10$
                                       $x = 5$

Take one x from both sides.

You are left with $2x$ only on the left-hand side.

If you need help, look back at page 139.

Exercise 12

Find the value of x in each problem.

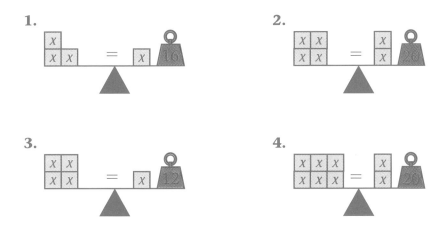

1.

2.

3.

4.

Exercise 13

Find the value of x in each problem.

1. $3x = x + 8$ **2.** $3x = x + 12$ **3.** $4x = 2x + 16$
4. $9x = 7x + 6$ **5.** $5x = 2x + 6$ **6.** $6x = 3x + 15$
7. $7x = 4x + 9$ **8.** $5x = x + 12$ **9.** $10x = 6x + 20$
10. $8x = 4x + 24$ **11.** $9x = 4x + 10$ **12.** $10x = 5x + 30$
13. $10x = 5x + 25$ **14.** $7x = 5x + 2$ **15.** $13x = 7x + 18$

REVIEW 4

A. SHAPE

rectangle   triangle   hexagon   octagon   circle

Count how many of each shape you can find in the three diagrams below.

1.   **2.**   **3.**

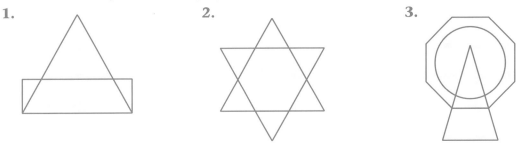

B. Measuring

1. The picture shows four mountains. Use the scale on the right to name them all.

Mount Snowdon is 1085 m high.
Scafell Pike is 978 m high.
Ben Nevis is 1343 m high.
Carrauntual is 1041 m high.

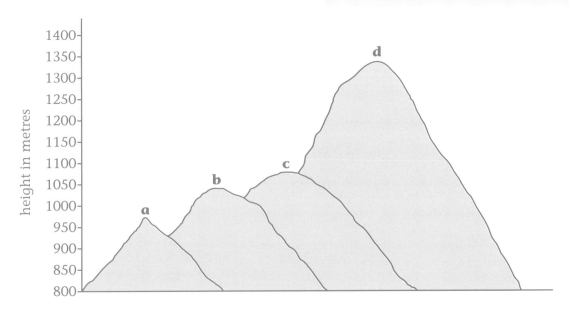

2. Copy and complete the following.

   a The world's longest tandem bicycle is over 20 ___ long.
      (centimetres – hours – metres – miles)

   b The world's longest river is the Nile and is 6670 ___ long.
      (millimetres – kilometres – months – centimetres)

   c A man once ate 144 prunes in 54 ___ to establish a record.
      (days – kilometres – seconds – hours)

   d The Earth takes about 365 ___ to go once around the Sun.
      (years – months – weeks – days)

   e A 2p piece is about 2 ___ thick.
      (metres – millimetres – hours – centimetres)

C. AREA

1. What is the area of each of these three shapes? Write down your answer in centimetre squares.

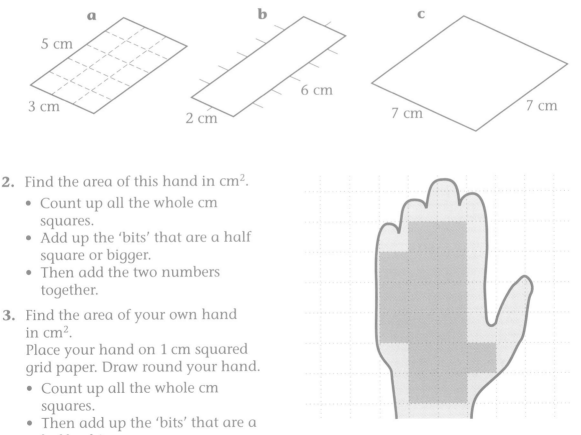

a
5 cm
3 cm

b
6 cm
2 cm

c
7 cm   7 cm

2. Find the area of this hand in cm².

- Count up all the whole cm squares.
- Add up the 'bits' that are a half square or bigger.
- Then add the two numbers together.

3. Find the area of your own hand in cm².
Place your hand on 1 cm squared grid paper. Draw round your hand.

- Count up all the whole cm squares.
- Then add up the 'bits' that are a half or bigger.
- Then add the two numbers together.

D. TIME AND DISTANCE

The time/distance graph shows the journey of a coach.

1. How many kilometres did the coach travel in 45 minutes?
2. How far did the coach travel during the first 20 minutes?
3. How long did the coach stop for?
4. How long did the coach take to travel the first 40 kilometres?
5. How far did the coach travel during the last 15 minutes?

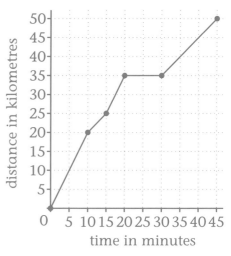

E. FRACTIONS

1. There were 20 people in a room. If half of them left, how many stayed?
2. There are 16 cats and dogs in a house. One quarter of them were dogs. How many cats were there?
3. There were 24 cakes in a shop. If half of them were sold, how many were left?
4. There were 20 cars in a car park. A quarter of them were red. How many red cars were there?
5. Jenny had 30p. She spent half of it. How much had she left?
6. What fraction of each shape is shaded?

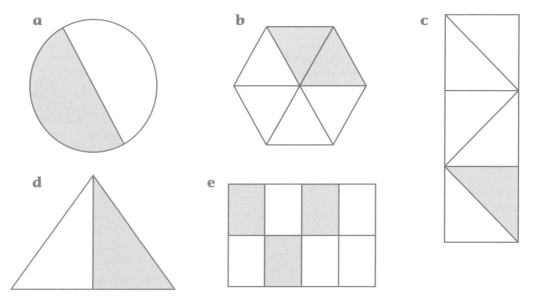

F. MATHS WORDS

Use the words in the box to complete these statements.

> hexagon   radius   circumference
>
> square   hour   triangle   quarter   octagon   day
>
> multiplication   division   half

1. ÷, this operation sign stands for _____.
2. When you share a cake into four equal parts, each fraction is a _____.
3. A _____ is a shape with three sides.
4. Sixty minutes are equal to one _____.
5. When you share a cake into two equal parts, each fraction is a _____.
6. An _____ is an eight-sided shape.
7. A six-sided shape is called a _____.
8. The distance from the middle of a circle to the edge is called the _____.
9. The unit to measure area is the _____.
10. There are 24 hours in one _____.
11. ×, this operation sign stands for _____.
12. The distance once around the edge of a circle is called the _____.

G. CONGRUENCE

Which images below are congruent to image **a**?

H. NUMBER PATTERN

Give one factor pair for each number in the factor trees below.

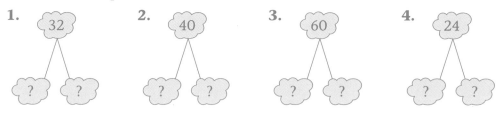

1. 32   **2.** 40   **3.** 60   **4.** 24

Find three factor pairs for each of these numbers.

5. 28   **6.** 36   **7.** 45   **8.** 50

Find the two prime numbers in each list below.

9. 2,4,5,6,8   **10.** 3,7,10,15   **11.** 10,4,11,17

12. Copy this list of numbers and underline the 'square numbers'.
1, 3, 4, 5, 7, 9, 12, 16, 20, 25, 28, 30, 42, 44, 49

I. ALGEBRA

Simplify these expressions. The first one is done for you.

1. $6a + 16a = 22a$ **2.** $2a + 3a + 5a =$ **3.** $7x + 9x + 2x =$

4. $20y + 16y - 8y =$ **5.** $15f + 20f - 9f =$ **6.** $4a + 2b + a + 5b =$

7. $14p + q + q + 3q =$ **8.** $21s + 2s + 3t + 15t =$ **9.** $3n + 5m + 14m + 18n =$

10. Find the value of x in each question.

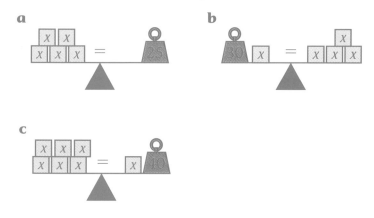

a

b

c

Find the value of the letters in the problems.

11. $2x = 24$ **12.** $5a = 35$ **13.** $3y = 45$

14. $4b = 28$ **15.** $4t = 80$ **16.** $5f = 45$

17. $6p = 54$ **18.** $2x = x + 10$ **19.** $3p = p + 10$

20. $5r = 2r + 18$ **21.** $7t = 3t + 20$ **22.** $6t = 4t + 50$

J. MIXED PROBLEMS

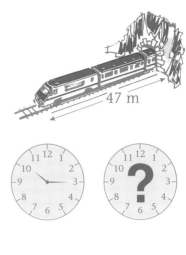

47 m

1. This train is 135 m long.
   How much of the train is still in the tunnel?

2. Alice has a paper round. She earns £7 a week.
   How many weeks will she have to work to
   earn £49?

3. If it is now 10.15, what time will it be in
   25 minutes time?

4. Measure these lines accurately.

5. If you get 25 cans of lemonade in a case, how many cans would you get in 6
   cases?

6. What is the next number in these number patterns?
   a 2,8,14,20,__   **b** 1,9,17,25,__   **c** 5,12,19,26,__

7. How many 10p pieces are there in £1.30?

8. How many 2p pieces are there in 38p?

9. A piece of string 48 cm long is cut into four equal pieces. How long is each
   piece?

10. How many tiles are covered by these objects?

    a

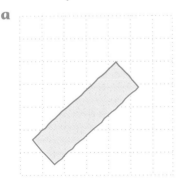

    b

11. This is a counter at a football ground turnstile.

    What will the counter read if one more person goes through the turnstile?

19 STREET MATHS 2

NUMERACY **BUYING A BICYCLE**

Joey tried to save up to buy a new bike.
Joey's newspaper round paid him £9 a
week, but he spent some of this.

Exercise 1

This is Joey's record of his weekly spending and saving.
Copy and complete the table.

week	earnings	spent	saved
1	£9	£3.00	
2	£9	£2.00	
3	£9	£5.50	
4	£9	£1.00	
5	£9	£0.50	
6	£9	£0.75	
7	£9	£3.25	
8	£9	£2.75	
9	£9	£4.25	
10	£9	£1.00	
		total	

Answer these questions using the table.

1. In which week did Joey spend most of his earnings?
2. In which week did Joey save most of his earnings?
3. In which two weeks did Joey save the same amount of money?
4. How much did Joey save in the first five weeks?
5. How much did Joey save in the last five weeks?
6. How much did Joey earn altogether?
7. How much did Joey save altogether?
8. Joey's father made the amount up to £132. How much money did his father give him?

Joey has £132 to spend.
He goes to two bicycle shops and collects their price lists
of racing bikes.

Rapid Bikes Ltd		41 High St.
RACING BIKES SALE		
	Normal price	Reduced by
B.R.R. Racer X10	£112	£10
Racer Rapide	£116	£15
Sim's Freewheeler	£130	£8
Super Ace 55	£185	£12
Clubman 99	£158	£23
Champion	£150	£25

Robinson and Sons	151 Church St.	
RACER SALE		Sale price
Super Ace 55	£188	£170
Speed King	£130	£120
Champion	£145	£120
Racer Rapide	£110	£99
Clubman 99	£149	£130
Road Star	£159	£145
B.R.R. Racer X10	£110	£99.99

Exercise 2

1. Make a list of the bikes Joey can afford with £132.
2. Which shop offers the best prices?
3. Joey decides to buy the *Champion* bike.
   a At which shop would he buy it?
   b After buying the bike, how much money has he
      left over?
4. What is the sale price of the *Clubman 99* at
   Rapid Bikes?
5. What is the sale price of the *Racer Rapide* at
   Rapid Bikes?
6. What is the sale price of the *Super Ace 55* at
   Rapid Bikes?
7. How much less is the sale price of the *Super Ace 55*
   at Robinsons?
8. How much can be saved on the *Racer Rapide*
   at Robinsons?

After buying his bike, Joey has £12 left. However, he still has to buy several more items for his bike. Here is the list.

One front light.
One back light.
Puncture repair kit.
Padlock and chain.

He goes shopping, and here is a selection of the items he needs.

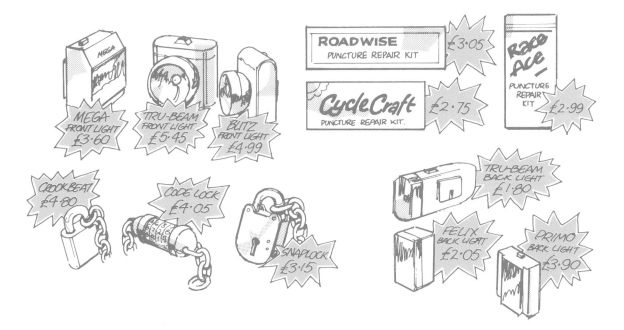

Exercise 3

1. How much does Joey spend if he buys the items he needs at the cheapest prices?
2. How much change from £12 would he have after buying them?
3. If he bought the most expensive front light and back light, how much would he spend?
4. How much is the dearest puncture repair kit?
5. How much is the dearest front light?
6. How much is the cheapest padlock and chain?
7. Which back light costs £2.05?
8. If Joey bought a Tru-Beam front light, and a Code Lock padlock and chain, how much would he spend?
9. If Joey bought a Primo back light and a Road Wise repair kit, how much would he spend?
10. If Joey bought a Blitz front light and a Crook Beat padlock and chain, how much would he spend?

NUTS AND BOLTS

Exercise 4

Here is a collection of hexagonal nuts from Joey's bike.
Using a ruler, find out which spanner fits which nut.

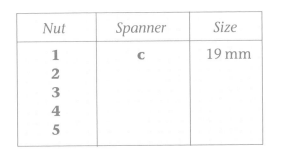

Nut	Spanner	Size
1	c	19 mm
2		
3		
4		
5		

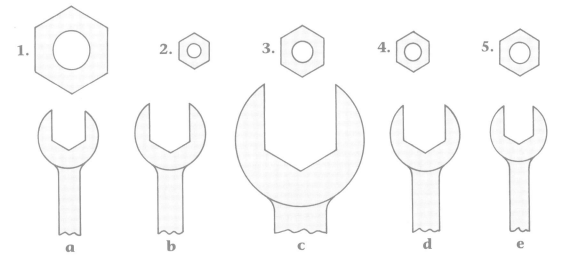

Exercise 5

Use a ruler to decide which nut fits which bolt.

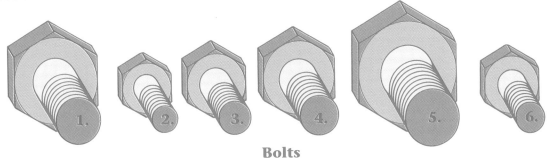

Bolts

Draw up a table to show your answers.

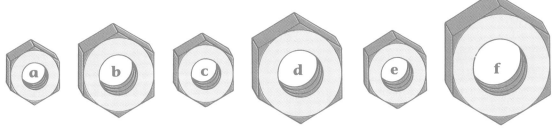

Nuts

The distance between each marker on the map below is 10 kilometres.
The distance from Joey's home to marker B is 20 kilometres.

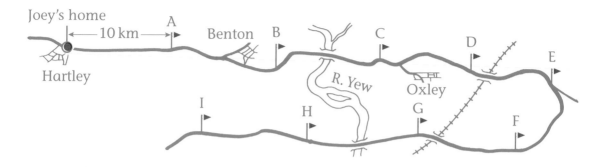

Exercise 6

1. Copy and complete these sentences.
    a The distance from Joey's home to marker C is ____ kilometres.
    b The distance from Joey's home to marker F is ____ kilometres.
    c The distance from Joey's home to marker I is ____ kilometres.
    d The distance from Joey's home to marker E is ____ kilometres.
2. Joey cycles 10 kilometres in one hour. How many hours will it take to cycle
    a from home to marker A   **b** from home to marker B
    c from home to marker D   **d** from home to marker F
    e from home to marker H   **f** from home to marker G?

Exercise 7

Answer the questions below for each of these three speedometers.

a    **b**   **c**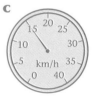

1. What speed is shown on Joey's speedometer?
2. How long would it take him to cycle 30 kilometres at this speed?
3. How long would it take him to cycle 60 kilometres at this speed?
4. If Joey left his home and cycled at this speed for 3 hours, which marker would he reach on the map above?

Exercise 8

If Joey cycles at 20 kilometres per hour, what distance would he cover in these times?

1. 1 hour   2. 2 hours   3. 4 hours   4. $\frac{1}{2}$ hour   5. $1\frac{1}{2}$ hours

6. $3\frac{1}{2}$ hours   7. 6 hours   8. $2\frac{1}{2}$ hours   9. $5\frac{1}{2}$ hours   10. $\frac{1}{4}$ hour

ON THE OPEN ROAD

Exercise 9

Here is a map showing part of Joey's journey.
During the journey he sees a number of road signs. Match the number on the map with a sign.

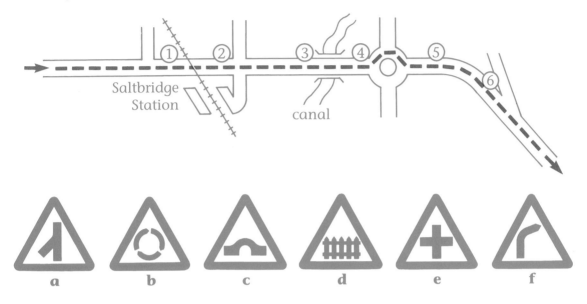

Exercise 10

Here is a map of Joey's journey.

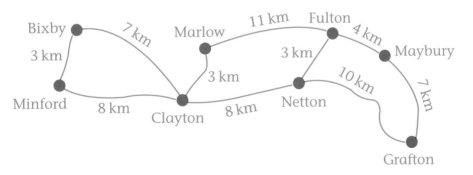

1. Joey starts at Minford, and cycles to Clayton and on to Netton. How far does he travel?
2. From Netton he cycled to Fulton, Maybury and Grafton. How far did he travel?
3. He then cycled to Bixby. How many kilometres is the shortest route?
4. How far is the shortest route between Minford and Fulton?
5. How far is the shortest route between Maybury and Clayton?
6. How far is the shortest route between Marlow and Grafton?

CYCLING COMPETITION

It is Saturday and Joey is taking part in a cycling competition.
All competitors are timed over three laps of the course.
The quickest time over three laps wins.

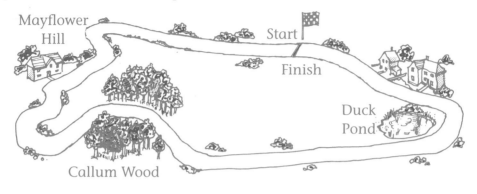

Exercise 11

Add up the times of these competitors and answer the questions below.

Toby Carson 19			Ruth Maddocks 27			Joey Greg 31			Mike Hill 22		
	Minutes	Seconds		Minutes	Seconds		Minutes	Seconds		Minutes	Seconds
Lap 1	1	. 20	Lap 1	1	. 30	Lap 1	1	. 32	Lap 1	1	. 18
Lap 2	2	. 12	Lap 2	2	. 05	Lap 2	2	. 09	Lap 2	2	. 35
Lap 3	2	. 26	Lap 3	2	. 18	Lap 3	2	. 10	Lap 3	2	. 41

Remember: 60 seconds equal 1 minute.

1. Who did the fastest first lap?
2. Who did the fastest second lap?
3. Who did the fastest last lap?
4. How long did Joey take to do the three laps?
5. How long did Ruth take to do the three laps?
6. How long did Toby take to do the three laps?
7. How long did Mike take to do the three laps?
8. Who came first, second, third and fourth?
9. Who took 2 minutes and 5 seconds to complete the second lap?
10. How long did the slowest lap take?